The Genesis Of Lincoln

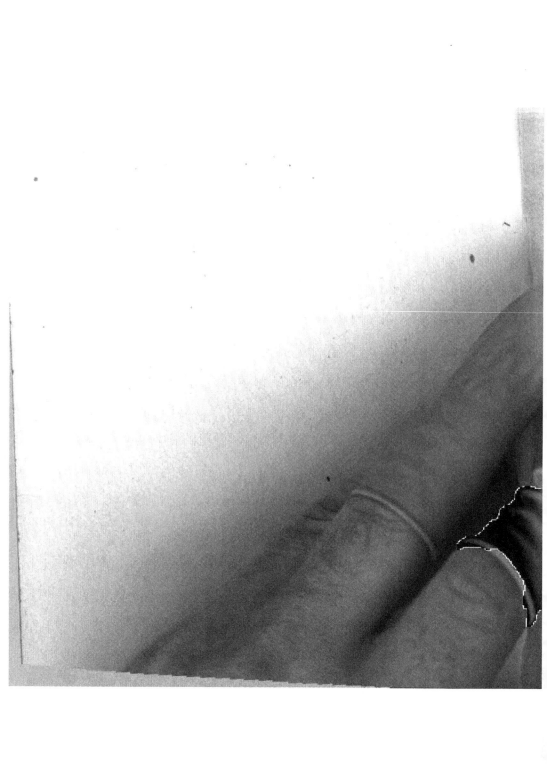

A Lincoln

JAMES H. CATHEY.

THE GENESIS OF LINCOLN.

BY

JAMES H. CATHEY.

Truth is Stranger Than Fiction.

"'I AM GLAD YOU HAVE UNDERTAKEN THE 'LINCOLN MYSTERY', IF SUCH IT CAN BE STYLED. I BE-LIEVE ALL THAT I HAVE HEARD."

—*The late Col. Jno. D. Cameron.*

"*He was, in the most significant way, a man who embodied all the best qualities of unspoiled middle-class men.*"

HENRY WARD BEECHER.

"The Characteristic which struck me most was his superabundance of common sense."

CHAUNCEY M. DEPEW.

"*There have indeed been times when such patriots as Garibaldi, Kossuth, and Lincoln have kindled in men an enthusiasm akin to adoration and worship.*"

NEWELL DWIGHT HILLIS.

"It is an unquestioned fact that Nancy Hanks was an inmate of Abraham Enloe's home, and that while there she became enceinte and went to Kentucky."

CAPT. JAS. W. TERRELL.

"*The people in this country—all the old people with whom I talked—were familiar with the girl as Nancy Hanks.*"

CAPT. E. EVERETT.

Dedication.

TO THE FUTURE BIOGRAPHER WHO MAY SEARCH FOR
ALL THE FACTS, AND THE COMING GENERA-
TIONS WHO MAY WANT THE WHOLE TRUTH,
THIS TRADITION OF ABRAHAM LINCOLN'S
ORIGIN, IS SINCERELY DEDICATED.

CONTENTS.

INDEX TO ILLUSTRATIONS

FOREWORD.

Generous reader, traverse with me the ensuing pages and they shall open to you a "sealed book." They shall lead along the neglected path of unwritten history and reveal to you, with care, an interesting fact in the story of America's most remarkable man.

They may tear the veil of popular modesty only to discover the naked truth.

The truth cannot hurt the living or the dead.

It is often a good popular nervine to disturb the commonplace with the heroic, the romantic, the tragic.

It is better still to replace popular shadow of doubt with popular sunshine of fidelity.

It is said, "there is a skeleton in every closet and that must not be disturbed." There

is no avoiding it with individuals or aggrega-
tions.

There should be no attempt to avoid explor-
ing the dimmest recesses in the life of a real
hero. The life and acts of a hero are not cir-
cumscribed by narrow lines. The atmosphere
that belongs to him at once becomes free and
self-imparting. Each and every phase of him
is of the intensest interest to humanity; at
once becomes, and of right should become, a
common heritage.

Tradition is the musty old closet in which
has been stowed for thousands of years the
disjoined skeletons of history. These should
be hauled forth, articulated, clothed with the
flesh, and animated with the blood of the living
truth.

There is one narrative of human events in
which there is no evidence of a traditional
closet—the Bible. In this ancient bundle of
truth "a spade is called a spade."

If the "man after God's own heart" took his

fellow's life that he might obtain his wife, this book says so in so many blunt words. If the "father of the faithful" drove his bond-woman and their illegitimate son into the wilderness to die, to please his irate wife, such is the record.

But it is not our purpose here to try to reconcile moral incongruities. It should be sufficient for one to reflect that our world is inhabited by *men*; that it *has* been so and doubtless will.

Yielding to a moral cowardice—a feeling that recoils at the thought of making public one's own faults—historians have, with a few refreshing exceptions, cast aside one-half the events of the world.

The custom to pass unnoticed the vices, which make up the larger moiety of the man, has lead them to an immoderate exaggeration of his virtues.

To these, and a false notion of taste, is traceable the failure to record volumes without

number of the most thrilling history. **Here**
is the trysting-place of truant tradition **and**
family lore. Here, too, is a fruitful nursery
of individual and national hypocrisy.

The recording of the good, only, in the life
of a person or a nation, is a tale half told, a
song half sung—often a wondrous tale, an epic
song.

The statue is not complete till the sculptor
has watched the last minute characteristic of
the original follow the errand of his chisel.
The flower does not show forth all its delicate tints in rounded splendor till its last tender petal is full blown.

Cicero tells us that the first and fundamen-
tal law of history is, " That it should neither
dare to say anything that is false or fear to say
anything that is true, nor give any just suspicion of favor or disaffection."

This is the standard of the true historian.
Apropos to this, Edward Everett Hale says:
" The history of mankind is made up of the

biographies of men." If this be true, Cicero's standard will apply to biography with double force.

The scriptural narrative traces the lineage of Christ along a solid chain of forty-two generations. If the sacred chronicler essayed to trace, without trepidation, so remote an origin as that of the divine Christ, why should one tremble or hesitate to inquire after the beginning of a great, though finite man? The day of miracles has passed these eighteen hundred years, and something cannot come of nothing.

It is the historical teaching that Abraham Lincoln was virtually "without ancestors, fellows, or successors." Whether this is a delusion it does not concern us to argue. He came into the world, and the world understood him not.

It is, therefore, the sole purpose of this little book to present a tradition tending to prove that this wonderful man was not without ancestors. His mother was Nancy Hanks. If.

he was the son of a worthy sire the world is entitled to know who that sire was; when, where and how he lived; whence he came and what his characteristics.

For ninety years, or thereabout, from the time it is said Abraham Lincoln was begotten or born, as the case was, and the breeze occurred in the Enloe home, there has subsisted among the honest people at the center of authority a lively tradition that Abraham, the head of the Enloe family, was Lincoln's father by Nancy Hanks, who occupied the position of servant-girl in the Enloe household.

So confident and persistent have the keepers of this old testimony to the origin of Abraham Lincoln been, when plied with interrogatories, that they knew what they were talking about, that there was no opening for superstition, and the most one who was inclined to be skeptical could do was to wonder and say nothing.

One might hug his incredulity by imagining that the people who fathered the strange accounts of Nancy Hanks and Abraham Enloe and a child, and the wonderful story of the striking personal likeness of Abraham Lincoln and Wesley Enloe, are illiterate, fanatical folk who have conjured up a fragmentary fable, how and for what they know not; but this incredulity is all cleared away, like fog before the sunbeams, when one learns that the custodians of the "Lincoln tradition" are numbered by the scores and hundreds of the first people— men and women—of Western North Carolina.

Ladies as well as gentlemen, not only of the immediate section, but also of distant States, visiting at Asheville and other places of resort in our mountains, finding a thread of the tradition, they pulled until their curiosity, at least, becoming excited, they visited Wesley Enloe, the alleged half-brother of Abraham Lincoln, in his hospitable mountain home, were filled with amazement, and went away convinced that the tradition was wrought in cords that could not easily be broken.

People who were familiar with Mr. Lincoln's history, or who knew _him personally, were struck with the strange physical resemblance on first sight, and then watched a series of impersonations of Lincoln, as they studied the features and noted the varying postures of the person of Wesley Enloe.

The remarkable tradition, with its flesh and blood corroboration, was from time to time engaged to be written up by journalists, lawyers and clergymen of culture and standing, but nothing more than a hasty, desultory newspaper article was the result. The people over a very limited area of population were being made conversant with the valuable tradition, and its worthy repositors were, one by one, stepping from the earthly stage. It was plainly apparent that in a very few years the old generation would be gone, and a truth of American history, by sheer neglect, would be forever lost.

We felt our incapacity to undertake so

responsible a task. We were conscious of the delicacy of the undertaking, but the implicit, unquestioned faith which we had in the truthfulness of the tradition gave us a courage which shrank not from the most formidable-looking anti-traditional hobgoblin.

Thus emboldened we set to work to gather the odds and ends of our folk-history. We resolved at the outset that we would interrogate none but the most trustworthy—people who were in the best position to give a reason for the faith that was in them, together with the story of the relatives of the distinguished subject of our memoir. This we have, in every instance, done. In 1895 the writer conceived the idea of writing a newspaper or magazine article for the simple purpose of making known the tradition to the public generally, hoping thereby to attract the attention of the enterprising journalist, and after that the enduring chronicler; but private concerns interfered, and our purpose was frustrated for the time. Luckily, however, we then obtained the statements of some very aged gentlemen whose testimony will herein appear, and which is of the most important character, who have since died.

We have been extremely fortunate in enlisting the co-operation of various good and often distinguished citizens in our search for data. Some of these have passed away since we began our first investigation. Those who are "up and able to be about" are the venerable half-brother of our illustrious subject, Mr. Wesley M. Enloe, and his nephew, Capt. Wm. A. Enloe; Dr. Isaac N. Enloe, of Illinois, and Mr. Sam. G. Enloe, of Missouri; Mr. J. Frank Enloe, of North Carolina, and Mrs. Floyd, of Texas, son and neice of Wesley M. Enloe; Mr. H. J. Beck, of Ocona Lufta, N. C.; C. A. Ragland, Esq., of Stockton, Mo.; Mr. Joseph A. Collins, of Clyde, N. C.; Capt. E. Everett, and Mr. D. K. Collins, of Bryson City, N. C.; the venerable Philip Dills, Hon. William A. Dills, and Mr. Sion T. Early, of Dillsboro, N. C.; and Captain James W. Terrell, of Webster, N. C.

To each of these gentlemen, and to Mrs. Floyd, the writer wishes to express his most sincere thanks. He has been most deeply touched by the generous and always courteous response his appeals have met from each and all of them, and his obligation to them can only be enhanced by the increase of the importance of the historical truth as it goes into the world fresh from their honest and disinterested lips. In voicing the memory of hundreds, these several individuals will, for the first time, bring face to face with the world a fact that is worth the world's while.

Tradition once said: "Premature pangs seized the mother of Napoleon while she was at church. She hurried home, barely reaching her apartment when the heroic babe was delivered, without accoucheur, on a piece of tapestry inwrought with an effigy of Achilles." Gradually becoming credulous, history says now: "This probably occurred."

There is not current a tradition of the

Corsican that is entitled to more credit than
the North Carolina tradition of the Immortal
Rail-splitter. We therefore give it to you
and the future historian, as you have it, in
modest but faithful form.

JAMES H. CATHEY.

Sylva, N. C.

CHAPTER I.

AN EXTRAORDINARY CASE.

In the year 1444, the story goes, Charles VII. of France, a man of forty, became suddenly and deeply enamored of a young Frenchwoman of not more than half his years, but more than twice his tact; and one of the brightest, wittiest, and most beautiful of women.

For six long years this nymph of grace and mischief kept King Charles wound tightly in her web of irresistible charms.

She caused him to neglect his most excellent consort, the queen, and her children; to place implacable hatred in the heart of Louis, the king's son, toward his father.

She beguiled him to provide her with regal

palaces throughout his realm; adorn her with the most costly apparel and bedeck her with the rarest jewels; to have her attended by long retinues of liveried servants and trained courtiers. She presented the king with bright and beautiful children; he adored Agnes Sorel with the wild intensity of a youthful lover, and the proud court of France, on bended knee, made obeisance to her.

At the end of the six years she suddenly died. The affair was first the property of gossip, then of tradition.

For many years the story of Charles and Agnes was passed from mouth to mouth.

Tales of her exquisite beauty and charms were familiar to prince and peasant. The secret of her beauty and attractions was said to have been her blond hair and teeth of rarest pearl, adorned at her will by the most bewitching smile.

As the years continued and the world hearkened to these seemingly extravagant reports, there might have been seen significant tossings of the head, and there might have been heard the murmurings of an incredulous public. But in the year 1777, three hundred and twenty-seven years after Charles the Seventh had gently laid Agnes in her tomb at Loches, it was decided by some ecclesiastics that her monument was in the way and that it must be removed. The monument was accordingly torn down, the marble slab was raised, and at a distance of a few feet in the ground the workman struck a coffin, the lid of which was taken away, then another of lead, which, when opened, disclosed a third of iron, inside of which they found a jaw filled with rows of shapely teeth, and long, flowing braids of blond hair soft as velvet. Since this it is said that no Frenchman has dared doubt the popular story of the personal beauty of Agnes Sorel.

This story of the king's mistress is a demonstration of the substantial truth of any deep-rooted tradition.

Illustrated thus tradition becomes what in fact it always is, a loud panegyric to the collective veracity of mankind. From out the shafted grave of human charity and the iron casket of canonization shall come forth the teeth and tresses of convincing testimony.

Tradition is the principal means by which plain people preserve a knowledge of events. History is made up of tradition. A very small percentage of the happenings of the world is recorded, the historian being an eye-witness. Even those events that are recorded when they take place are anticipated, being of the most important character, and become the subjects of a score of chroniclers, all embalming the same substantial facts, but immersed in the peculiar oils and spices of each individual chronicler.

Many of the most delicate and yet indispensable notes of history that tell of the real character of people, savage and savant, come down the decades by word of mouth. They are passed from ear to ear in silent pride and childish confidence around the cozy firesides of neighborhoods and states.

It is the inestimable and inalienable right of memory.

Deprive, if it were possible, a people of their traditions, and you will rob memory of the tenderer half of its trophies. You will transform joyous youth into sober manhood in a single night, and turn the sunny plain of the aged into a wailing desert in a single day.

Every long-established and generally accepted tradition bears upon its face the authority of truth. The popular gaze melts away the mist, and popular scrutiny finds out the facts; popular judgment weighs these facts, and popular honesty discloses them.

The birth and many of the events in the life of Christ were for a long while confided to tradition's sacred keeping. Now that they are written in books and chiseled in marble, who doubts the tale of the shepherds and admissions of the wise men?

The birth and life of Christ carry with them divine authorization. So does-any truth.

The following tradition is more than ninety years old. Its center of authority is Swain and neighboring counties of Western North Carolina :

Some time in the early years of the century, variously given 1803, 1805, 1806, and 1808, there was living in the family of Abraham Enloe, of Ocona Lufta, N. C., a young woman whose name was Nancy Hanks. This young woman remained in the household, faring as one of the family until, it becoming apparent that she was in a state of increase, and there appearing signs of the approach of domestic infelicity, she was quietly removed, at the instance of Abraham Enloe, to Kentucky.

This is the most commonly accepted version of the event.

Another pretty current construction of the story is that when Abraham Enloe emigrated irom Rutherford county, there came with his family a servant-girl whose name was Nancy Hanks, and who, after a time, gave birth to a boy child which so much resembled the legitimate heirs of Abraham Enloe, that their mother warmly objected to the presence of so unpleasant a reminder, and the embarrassed husband had the young child and its mother spirited to Kentucky. These are the two universally accepted versions of the one thoroughly accredited fact.

The tradition subsists on four salient and perfectly conversant points:

First.—That in the early years of the century a young woman took up her abode at Abraham Enloe's, in the capacity of hired girl, whose name was Nancy Hanks.

Second.——That this same girl, Nancy Hanks, while living at Abraham Enloe's, became *enceinte ;* or entangled in an embarrassment in which her illegitimate child was the unconscious instigator.

Third.—That the wife of Abraham Enloe,

believing that her husband was the father of Nancy Hanks's child, and being unwilling to countenance what she conceived to be a reproach upon herself and children, demanded the disconnection of Nancy Hanks from her household.

Fourth.—That Abraham Enloe heeded the demand of his wife and forthwith effected the transportation of Nancy Hanks and her offspring to the State of Kentucky.

" Wherefore she said unto Abraham, cast out the bondwoman and her son, for the son of this bondwoman shall not be heir with my son, even with Isaac.

And the thing was very grievous in Abraham's sight because of his son.

And God said unto Abraham, Let it not be grievous in thy sight because of the lad, and because of thy bondwoman; in all that Sarah hath said unto thee, hearken unto her voice; for in Isaac shall thy seed be called.

And also of the son of the bondwoman will I make a nation, because he is thy seed.

And Abraham rose up early in the morning and took bread and a bottle of water, and gave it unto Hagar, putting it on her shoulder, and the child, and sent her away; and she departed and wandered in the wilderness of Beersheba.

And the water was spent in the bottle, and she cast the child under one of the shrubs. And she went and sat her down over against him a good way off, as it were a bow-shot; for she said let me not see the death of the child. And she sat over against him and lifted up her voice and wept.

And God heard the voice of the lad; and the angel of God called to Hagar out of heaven and said unto her: What aileth thee, Hagar? fear not; for God has heard the voice of the lad where he is. Arise, lift up the lad and hold him in thine hand; for I will make him a great nation.

And God opened her eyes and she saw a well of water; and she went and filled the bottle with water and gave the lad drink.

And God was with the lad, and he grew and
dwelt in the wilderness, and became an archer.
And he dwelt in the wilderness of Paran."

This is the entire beautiful and pathetic
story of Hagar and her son. As one reads it
how much of it seems analogous to poor
Nancy Hanks and the account of Abraham
Lincoln's childhood.

But if men and women living under kindred
circumstances a little more than three-quarters
of a century since are as much entitled to be
believed as Moses, the drama of Abraham
and Sarah and their bondwoman Hagar, and
her child, in this tradition, is again enacted
with strange fidelity. Bereft of the tender
guardianship of either father or mother, and
thrown adrift on the cold charity of the world,
Nancy Hanks, in what particular manner is
unknown at this distant day, sought shelter
under the kindly roof of Abraham Enloe.

She was young, doubtless yet in her teens.
The bloom of youth had not faded from her

THE OLD HOUSE.

The Residence of Wesley Enloe, and the House of Abraham Enloe when Nancy Hanks was Transported to Kentucky.

brow. The expression of native intelligence, saddened by scenes of poverty and pain, shone from her eye. In her voice ran a tone of melancholy, betraying a life of sorrow and neglect.

It was a red-letter day for her when she was welcomed by the family into the comfortable home of Abraham Enloe. Never had the sun shone brighter or the birds sung sweeter to her than on that day. She drank afresh life's invigorating elixir, and dreamed for the first time of some of its most pleasant realities.

Her face became changed; there was now no mingled look of weariness and woe, only a faint trace of the sad. Her eye was changed; there was now the sparkle of light and life, with the dimmest expression of gloom. Her voice was changed; there was now the music of contentment and peace, with the softest accompaniment of grief.

In a word, from the day Nancy Hanks entered the home of Abraham Enloe hers was the happy fortune for the first time in her life to know what was meant by having comfortable clothes, a good bed, nutritious food and warm friends, and ere she was aware rosy health and radiant hope had stolen into her being and taken up their abode.

She had now learned the formal round of household chores, and her life became halcyon. In her step was the light, quick spring of youth, and she turned off the domestic duties with a despatch and ease that would have done credit to one of more practiced skill.

Months, and it may be years, passed thus, and the cherry presence and admirable service of Nancy Hanks engrafted themselves into the family life and economy of Abraham Enloe; she was by mutual and inadvertent acknowledgment one of its members.

But the time came when the "even tenor" of Abraham Enloe's household was disturbed; it was a sly and impious mishap, for which the head of the household was held by his wife to be primarily responsible.

It was a sad hour when Nancy Hanks was forced by her mistake to take a final leave of her otherwise happy home in the Carolina mountains.

There is no doubt but that indirectly Abraham Enloe gave her the "bread and bottle of water" the morning she was sent into the forest and toward her Kentucky home. Nay, more, there is little doubt that he was better to her and his child than was Abraham of old to Hagar and his, for he did not set them adrift in the wilderness to survive or perish as it pleased providence, but like a man with a great compassionate heart, provided them horses and a safe consort to bring them to their predetermined destination.

However remarkable the similarity in physical circumstances, equally wonderful is the moral analogy of these two cases.

If the case of Hagar and her tender boy presents a picture of pity and despair, that of Nancy Hanks and her infant child presents a

scene that is the very soul of sorrow and re-
gret. The parallel does not cease with their
banishment and journeyings, but is sustained
in the privations and sufferings in childhood
and youth, and the exalted honor and distinc-
tion of the mature manhood of Ishmael and
Abraham Lincoln.

Charles Kingsley says: "It was ordained,
ages since, into what particular spot each
grain of gold should be washed down from an
Australian quartz reef, that a certain man
might find it at a certain moment and crisis of
his life."

A learned divine recently said: "St John
wrote his gospels about sixty years after the
events took place. Yet he had an old man's
vivid recollection of distant occurrences."

Tendering them these words of assurance
from most eminent authority, we shall here
turn over this tradition, for the time being, to
its faithful repositors.

PHILIP DILLS.

Mr. Dills. was born in Rutherford county, N. C., January 10, 1808. His father emigrated to the mountains of Western North Carolina almost contemporaneously with Abraham Enloe. Although Mr. Dills was four years old when Jackson whipped Pakenham at New Orleans, he is nimble both in body and mind. He describes the removal of the Cherokees west of the Mississippi; tells of the elections when Clay and Jackson were rivals—of casting his first vote for the latter; recalls the personal appearance of John C. Calhoun, whom he saw and with whom he talked; the duel between Sam Carson and Dr. Vance, and many other incidents of early days he distinctly remembers and recites with genuine gusto.

Mr. Dills is a citizen of Jackson county. His post-office is Dillsboro. He said:

"Although a generation younger and living some twenty-five miles from him, I knew

Abraham Enloe personally and intimately.
I lived on the road which he frequently traveled in his trips south, and he made my house
a stopping-place. He was a large man, tall,
with dark complexion, and coarse, black hair.
He was a splendid looking man, and a man
of fine sense. His judgment was taken as a
guide, and he was respected and looked up to
in his time.

"I do not know when I first heard of his
relation with Nancy Hanks, but it was many
years before the civil war, and while I was a
very young man. The circumstance was
related in my hearing by the generation older
than myself, and I heard it talked over time
and again later. I have no doubt that Abraham Enloe was the father of Abraham Lincoln."

WALKER BATTLE.

Mr. Battle was born February 12, 1809, in
Haywood county. His father was one of
the three men who came to Ocona Lufta with

Abraham Enloe. He was a highly respected citizen of Swain county. The following statement was received from him in 1895. He has since died. His son, Milton Battle, a reputable citizen, is familiar with his father's statement. His post-office is Bryson City, N. C. Walker Battle said:

"My father was one of the first settlers of this country. He came here with Abraham Enloe. I have lived here my entire life, and I knew Abraham Enloe and his family almost as well as I knew my own.

"The incident occurred, of course, before my day, but I distinctly remember hearing my own family tell of the trouble between Abraham Enloe and Nancy Hanks when I was a boy. I recall, as if it were but yesterday, hearing them speak of Nancy's removal to Kentucky and that she married there a fellow by the name of Lincoln; that Abraham Enloe had some kind of correspondence with the woman after he sent her to Kentucky—

-sent her something—and that he had to be very cautious to keep his wife from finding it out.

"There is no doubt as to Nancy Hanks having once lived in the family of Abe Enloe, and there is no doubt that she was the mother of a child by him.

"No, I never saw Nancy Hanks's name in print in my life, and never saw a sketch of Abraham Lincoln, or heard of him, until he became a candidate for the presidency in 1860."

WILLIAM H. CONLEY.

Mr. Conley was born about the year 1812, in Haywood county. He lived the greater part of his life within fifteen miles of Abraham Enloe's. He was a man of intelligence and perfect veracity. The following statement, the original of which is in the writer's possession, was obtained from him in 1895. He has since died.

Mr. Conley said:

"My father, James Conley, was the first white man to settle on the creek in this (Swain) county, which bears his name. Abraham Enloe was one of the first to settle on Ocona Lufta. Enloe and my father were warm friends. I knew Abe Enloe myself well. He was an impressive looking man. On first sight you were compelled to think that there was something extraordinary in him, and when you became acquainted with him your first impression was confirmed. He was far above the average man in mind.

"As to the tradition: I remember when I was a lad, on one occasion some of the women of the settlement were at my father's house, and in conversation with my mother they had a great deal to say about some trouble that had once occurred between Abe Enloe and a girl they called Nancy Hanks, who had at some time staid at Enloe's. I heard nothing more, as I now remember, about the matter, until the year before the war, the news came that Abraham Lincoln had been nominated for the presidency, when it was the common understanding among the older people that Lincoln was the son of Abe Enloe by Nancy Hanks.

"Not one of them had ever seen, up to that time, a written account of Lincoln. There is no doubt that Nancy Hanks lived at Abraham Enloe's. She became pregnant while there by Abraham Enloe, and to quell a family disturbance Enloe had her moved to Kentucky, just as my father and mother, and others, have time and again related in my hearing.

"I have no doubt that Abe Enloe was the father of Abraham Lincoln."

CAPTAIN EP. EVERETT.

Captain Everett was born April 4, 1830, in Davy Crockett's native county, Tennessee. He came to what was then Jackson, now Swain county, in the late fifties, and has since lived in twelve miles of the Abe Enloe homestead. He was captain of Company E, Third

Tennessee. He served through the entire war, showing conspicuous courage at First Manassas. He helped to organize the county of Swain, in 1871. He was a member of the Constitutional Convention of 1875, that amended the Constitution of the State. He has been magistrate, mayor of the town of Bryson City, and sheriff of the county. He is well known throughout the State as one of her best and brainiest citizens. He said:

"In time of the war, in conversation with various old and reliable citizens of this section, I learned that Abe Lincoln's mother, Nancy Hanks, once lived in the family of Abe Enloe and was sent from there to Kentucky, to be delivered of a child. The cause of her removal to Kentucky was a threatened row between Abe Enloe and old Mrs. Enloe, his wife. The people in this county—all the old people with whom I talked—were familiar with the girl as *Nancy Hanks*. This subject was not only the common country rumor, but I saw it similarly

rehearsed in the local newspapers of the time.
I have no doubt of its truth."

CAPTAIN JAMES W. TERRELL.

Captain Terrell was born in Rutherford
county, N. C., the last day of the year 1829.
At the age of sixteen he came to Haywood,
where he lived with his grandfather, Wm. D.
Kirkpatrick, until 1852, when he joined himself in business with Col. Wm. H. Thomas, a
man of great shrewdness and enterprise. In
1854 he was made disbursing agent to the
North Carolina Cherokees. In 1862 he en-
listed in the Confederate service as lieutenant
in a company of Cherokee Indians. Later he
was promoted. Since the war he has mer-
chandised and been a railroad contractor. He
has represented his county in the legislature
and filled other offices of trust and honor. He
is recognized throughout Western North Carolina as a most excellent and useful citizen.
He said:

"Having personally had some hints from the Enloes, of Jackson and Swain, with whom I am intimately acquainted, my attention was seriously drawn to the subject by an article which appeared in *Bledsoe's Review*, in which the writer gives an account of a difficulty between Mr. Lincoln's reputed father and a man named Enloe.

"I then began to inquire into the matter and had no difficulty in arriving at the following indisputable facts, for which I am indebted to the following old people: The late Dr. John Mingus, son-in-law to Abraham Enloe; his widow Mrs. Polly Mingus, daughter of Abraham Enloe (lately deceased), and their son Abram Mingus, who still lives; also to the late William Farley and the late Hon. William H. Thomas, besides many other very old people, all of whom, I believe, are now dead.

"1st. Some time about the beginning of the present century, a young orphan girl was employed in the family of Abram Enloe, then of Rutherford county, N. C. Her position in the family was nearly that of member, she being an orphan with no relatives that she knew. *Her name was undoubtedly Nancy Hanks.* Abram Enloe moved about the year 1805 from Rutherford, stopping first for a short while on Soco creek, but eventually settled on the Ocona Lufta, where his son, Wesley M. Enloe, now resides, then Buncombe, afterward Haywood, later Jackson and now Swain county.

"2d. Some time after settling on the Ocona Lufta Miss Hanks became *enceinte*, and a family breeze resulted and Nancy Hanks was sent to Kentucky.

"3d. She was accompanied to Kentucky by or through the instrumentality of Hon. Felix Walker, then a member of Congress from the 'Buncombe district.'

"There is no doubt of the truth of these statements. They were all of them well known to a generation just passed away, and with many of whom I was well and intimately acquainted. The following I give as it came to me:

"A probable reason for sending the girl Nancy Hanks to Kentucky was that at that time some of the Enloe kindred were living there. I was informed that a report reached here that she was married soon after reaching Kentucky.

"Mrs. Abram Enloe's maiden name was Egerton, and she was a native of Rutherford county. Some years ago, meeting with Dr. Egerton, of Hendersonville, and finding that he was a relative of Mrs. Enloe, our conversation drifted toward the Enloe family, and he imparted to me the following:

"Some time in the early fifties two young men of Rutherford county moved to Illinois and settled in or near Springfield. One of them, whose name was Davis, became intimately acquainted with Mr. Lincoln. In the fall of 1860, just before the presidential election, Mr. Davis and his friend paid a visit back to Rutherford and spent a night with Dr. Egerton. Of course the presidential candidates would be discussed. Mr. Davis told Dr. Egerton that in a private and confidential talk which he had with Mr. Lincoln the latter told him that he was of Southern extraction, that his right name was, or ought to have been, Enloe, but that he had always gone by the name of his *stepfather*.

"Mr. Enloe's Christian name was Abram, and if Mr. Lincoln was his son he was not unlikely named for him.

"About the time of the famous contest between Lincoln and Stephen A. Douglass, Hon. Wm. H. Seward franked to me a speech of Mr. Lincoln's, made in that campaign, entitled: 'Speech of Hon. *Abram* Lincoln.' He himself invariably signed his name 'A. Lincoln.'

"To my mind, taking into consideration the unquestioned fact that Nancy Hanks was an inmate of Abram Enloe's family, that while there she became pregnant, that she went to Kentucky and there married an obscure man named Lincoln, the story is highly probable indeed, and when fortified with the wonderful likeness between Wesley M. Enloe, legitimate son of Abram Enloe, and Mr. Lincoln, I cannot resist the conviction that they are sons of the same sire. A photo of either might be passed on the family of the other as their genuine head."

HON. WM. A. DILLS.

Mr. Dills is a native of Jackson county, N. C., and resides in the thriving little town which was named in his honor—Dillsboro. He is an intelligent, progressive citizen. His people have honored him with place and power. He has represented his county in the lower house of the legislature. He said:

"My information with regard to the subject, so far as this country is concerned, is traditional, as the events named occurred long before I was born.

"Several years ago, while I was teaching school in the State of Missouri, I read a sketch of the life of Abraham Lincoln, which ran as follows: 'Abraham Lincoln was born in the State of Kentucky, of a woman whose name was Nancy Savage or Nancy Hanks. His father is supposed to have been a man by the name of Enloe. When the boy was eight years old his mother married an old man by the name of Lincoln, whose profession was rail-splitting. Soon after the marriage he took a large contract of splitting rails in the State of Illinois, where he took the boy and his mother, and the boy assumed the name of Lincoln.' The above is a verbatim quotation of the sketch that far.

"On my return from Missouri I took occasion to investigate the old tradition to my own satisfaction. I found that Nancy Hanks once lived with Abraham Enloe, in the county of

Buncombe (now Swain), and while there became involved with Enloe; a child was imminent, if it had not been born, and Nancy Hanks was conveyed to Kentucky.

"The public may read in Wesley M. Enloe, son of Abraham Enloe, a walking epistle of Abraham Lincoln. If there is any reliance to be placed in tradition of the strongest class they are half-brothers. I have not the shadow of a doubt the tradition is true.

"For further information, I refer you to Col. Allen T. Davidson, of Asheville."

JOSEPH A. COLLINS.

Mr. Collins is fifty-six years of age and resides in the town of Clyde, in Haywood county. He served three years of the war between the States as a private, after which he was promoted to the second lieutenancy of his company, in which capacity he continued until the surrender. He has been in the mercantile business for twenty-five years, ten years of which he was a traveling salesman. He is now proprietor of a hardware store in his home town. He is well known over the entire western part of the State as a gentleman of the most unquestionable integrity. He said:

"The first I knew of any tradition being connected with Abraham Lincoln's origin on his father's side was in 1867. At that time I was in Texas, and while there I made the acquaintance of Judge Gilmore, an old gentleman who lived three miles from Fort Worth.

"He told me he knew Nancy Hanks before she was married, and that she then had a child she called Abraham. 'While the child was yet small,' said Judge Gilmore, 'she married a man by the name of Lincoln, a whisky distiller. 'Lincoln,' he said, 'was a very poor man, and they lived in a small log house.'

"'After Nancy Hanks was married to the man Lincoln,' said Gilmore, 'the boy was known by the name of Abraham Lincoln. He said that Abraham's mother, when the boy was about eight years old, died.'

"Judge Gilmore said he himself was five or six years older than Abraham Lincoln; that he knew him well; attended the same school with him. He said Lincoln was a bright boy and learned very rapidly; was the best boy to work he had ever known.

"He said he knew Lincoln until he was almost grown, when he, Gilmore, moved to Texas. During his residence in Texas he was elected judge of the county court. He was an intelligent, responsible man.

"Years ago I was traveling for a house in Knoxville. On Turkey creek, in Buncombe county, N. C., I met an old gentleman whose name was Phillis Wells. He told me that he knew Abraham Lincoln was the son of Abraham Enloe, who lived on Ocona Lufta.

"Wells said he was then ninety years of age. When he was a young man he traveled over the country and sold tinware and bought furs, feathers, and ginseng for William Johnston, of Waynesville. He said he often stopped with

Abraham Enloe. On one occasion he called to stay over night, as was his custom, when Abraham Enloe came out and went with him to the barn to put up his horse, and while there Enloe said:

"'My wife is mad; about to tear up the place; she has not spoken to me in two weeks, and I wanted to tell you about it before you went in the house.' Then, remarked Wells: 'I said what is the matter?' and Abraham Enloe replied: 'The trouble is about Nancy Hanks, a hired girl we have living with us.' Wells said he staid all night, and that Mrs. Enloe did not speak to her husband while he was there. He said he saw Nancy Hanks there; that she was a good-looking girl, and seemed to be smart for business.

" Wells said before he got back there on his next trip that Abraham Enloe had sent Nancy Hanks to Jonathan's creek and hired a family there to take care of her; that later a child was born to Nancy Hanks, and she named him Abraham.

"Meantime the trouble in Abraham Enloe's family had not abated. As soon as Nancy Hanks was able to travel, Abraham Enloe hired a man to take her and her child out of the country, in order to restore quiet and peace at home. He said he sent her to some of his relatives near the State line between Tennessee and Kentucky. He said Nancy and the child were cared for by Enloe's relatives until she married a fellow by the name of Lincoln.

"I asked the old gentleman if he really believed Abraham Lincoln was the son of Abraham Enloe, and he replied: 'I know it, and if I did not know it I would not tell it.'

"I made special inquiry about the character of Wells, and every one said that he was an honest and truthful man and a good citizen."

H. J. BECK.

Mr. Beck was born and reared and has all his life lived on Ocona Lufta. He was one of Abraham Enloe's neighbors, as was his father before him. He is now an octogenarian. He

ıs well-to-do, intelligent and of upright character. He said :

" I have heard my father and mother often
speak of the episode of Abraham Enloe and
Nancy Hanks. They said Abraham Enloe
moved from Rutherford county here, bringing
with his family a hired girl named Nancy
Hanks. Some time .after they settled here
Nancy Hanks was found to be with child,
and Enloe procured Hon. Felix Walker to
take her away. Walker was gone two or
three weeks. If they told where he took her I
do not now think of the place.

"As to Abraham Enloe, he was a very large
man, weighing between two and three hundred.
He was justice of the peace. The first I remember of him, I was before him in trials.
In these cases, of difference between neighbors,
he was always for peace and compromise. If
an amicable adjustment could not be effected
he was firm and unyielding. He was an excellent business man."

D? K. COLLINS.

Mr. Collins was born October 8, 1844. He was a Lieutenant of Sharpshooters, Company F, 69th N. C. Regiment. He is the most extensive dry-goods merchant in the State west of Asheville. He is an excellent citizen and cultured gentleman. He said :

"The tradition is well-founded. I have been in position to note its bearings, and there is no doubt that Nancy Hanks lived at Abraham Enloe's, and that the event took place substantially as related by the men and women who were familiar with it."

CAPT. WM. A. ENLOE.

Captain Enloe was born in Haywood (now Jackson) county, and is sixty-six years of age. He is a successful merchant and business man. He is a gentleman of superior sense, modesty, firmness and integrity. He was Captain of Company F, 29th N. C. Regiment, commanded by Robt. B. Vance, and served through the war. He has represented his county in the

General Assembly. He ·is a grandson of Abraham Enloe. He said:

"There is a tradition come down through the family that Nancy Hanks, the mother of President Lincoln, once lived at my grandfather's, and while there became the mother of a child said to be my grandfather Abraham Enloe's.

One Mr. Thompson married my aunt Nancy, daughter of Abraham Enloe, contrary to the will of my grandfather; to conceal the matter from my grandfather's knowledge, Thompson stole her away and went to Kentucky; on the trip they were married. Hearing of their marriage, my grandfather reflected and decided to invite them back home. On their return they were informed of the tumult in my grandfather's household because of Nancy Hanks, who had given birth to a child; and when my uncle and aunt, Thompson and wife, returned to their Kentucky home, they took with them Nancy Hanks and her child. This is the family story as near as I can reproduce it from memory.

"In 1861 I came home from Raleigh to recruit my company. On my return, while waiting for the stage in Asheville, I took dinner at what was then the Carolina House. The table was filled largely with officers going to and from their various commands. The topic of conversation seemed to be Abraham Lincoln. One of the gentlemen remarked that Lincoln was not the correct name of the President— that his name was Enloe and that his father lived in Western North Carolina. I maintained the part of an interested listener, and no one suspected that my name was Enloe.

"After this, during the war, and while stationed in East Tennessee, I was handed a paper with nearly a column of what purported to be a sketch of Abraham Lincoln's early life in Kentucky—alleging that his father's name was Enloe, and that he (Lincoln) was born in Western North Carolina."

WESLEY M. ENLOE.

Mr. Enloe was born 1811, in Haywood county, N. C., and is the ninth and only surviving son of Abraham Enloe. He resides on the same farm and in the same house in which his father lived when Nancy Hanks was banished from the household. He is a quiet, suave, intelligent gentleman of the old school, and a prosperous farmer. He said:

"I was born after the incident between father and Nancy Hanks. I have, however, a vivid recollection of hearing the name Nancy Hanks frequently mentioned in the family while I was a boy. No, I never heard my father mention it; he was always silent on the subject so far as I know.

"Nancy Hanks lived in my father's family. I have no doubt the cause of my father's sending her to Kentucky is the one generally alleged. The occurrence as understood by my generation and given to them by that of my father, I have no doubt is essentially true.

WESLEY M. ENLOE.

Traditional Half-brother of Abraham Lincoln at the
Age of 88.

"My father moved to this place (Ocona Lufta) somewhere from 1803 to 1808."

A NEWSPAPER ARTICLE.

It has been our steady resolve to admit nothing in these memoirs over a fictitious or anonymous signature. But as all the newspaper articles on the subject available are thus signed, we determined to depart from our rule and give the full text of a correspondence in the *Charlotte Observer* of September 17th, 1893.

The Observer is one of the foremost public prints of the south. It is edited by Colonel Joseph P. Caldwell, a distinguished member of an old, distinguished family, and one of the most brilliant journalists in the country.

And if we have been rightly informed, the writer, who signs himself "Student of History," is a worthy member of another and illustrious North Carolina family.

To the Editor of The Observer :—My attention has been called to the communication in last Sunday's edition on Abraham Lincoln's

ancestry. The communication and your interesting editorial called to mind a true story in
the life of one of Lincoln's contemporaries,
Mr. Judah P. Benjamin. It is not known to
many of this generation that Mr. Benjamin,
when a boy, lived in Fayetteville, N. C., and
was a student in the academy, in that city.
His brother Solomon and his sister Judith,
when quite small, lived in the same town. I
think it is true, too, that a part of his boyhood
was spent in Wilmington, N. C. His family
were English Hebrews, and he was born in
the West Indies. Hon. Warren Winslow,
when in Congress, tried to remind Mr. Benjamin of his early life in North Carolina. I
heard him say he failed to make Mr. Benjamin's 'memory recollect.' His early life in
the United States began in North Carolina
and official life, as a member of Mr. Davis's
cabinet, ended in Greensboro, N. C., or Charlotte, in the same State. He separated from
Mr. Davis the morning after he left Washing-

ton, Ga. He was Lincoln's junior by two
years. Your correspondent connects Lincoln's
life with North Carolina.

A few years since, probably in 1889, the
writer of this communication was informed by
Dr. A. W. Miller that he heard in Western
North Carolina that there was a tradition in
Swain county that Abraham Lincoln was
born in that county. That his father's name
was Abram Enloe, and the name of his mother
was Nancy Hanks. That the house in which
he was born was at that time occupied by
Wesley Enloe, a son of Abram Enloe, and,
ergo, the half-brother of the great president.

In 1890, being in Webster, Jackson county,
I met a gentleman who was county surveyor
of Jackson, who gave me the story related by
Dr. Miller, and added facts in the tradition.
The story as related to the doctor was, that
Nancy Hanks and Abram were carried to
Kentucky by a mule-drover who was in the
habit of stopping at Abram Enloe's, at the

foot of the Smoky mountains, about 1804.
The surveyor's information was that Felix
Walker, the congressional representative—the
author of the famous expression 'speaking for
Buncombe'—in order to do his constituent
"A'bram" a good turn, carried Hagar and
Ishmael to Hardin county, Kentucky. He
stated also that two citizens, Davis by name,
lodged one night at his friend's house and
stated that they lived in Illinois, and had emigrated to that State from Rutherford county,
N. C. These gentlemen stated that Abraham
Lincoln was acquainted with them, and on
learning they were from Rutherford county,
told them his mother had frequently told him
she had lived in that county. These gentlemen informed their host (Dr. Egerton of
Hendersonville, I think) that Abram Lincoln
was one of the big men of the great west, from
which they had hailed. This incident happened about 1858.

The following week the writer was in
Bryson City.

Dr. Miller was under the impression that
Wesley Enloe was a facsimile of Abraham
Lincoln, or certain members of the Enloe
family were very similar in features to
him. The Jackson surveyor had excited my
curiosity, and, having a day off, I lost no
time, and was soon on my route up the
Tuckaseegee, bound for the Abram Enloe
homestead, just fourteen miles from Bryson
City. The road was rocky, and my driver
was of the silent kind, so I gave my attention
to the shaping of my interview on what
loomed up to me as a very difficult subject to
handle. A silence of five miles was suddenly
interrupted by the driver's inquiry as to my
business with Mr. Wesley Enloe. I replied
promptly, "I am going up principally to look
at him." This answer left me to my own
reflections and the scenery of the Ocona Lufta,
a branch of the Tuckaseegee, which is beautiful beyond description. The native Indian
sunned himself along the roadside, or paddled

his smooth canoe under the overhanging
Rhododendron. Suddenly the driver, over-
burdened with curiosity, at the ninth mile-
stone, interrupted me with the question,
"Would I mind telling what I wanted to look
at Wesley Enloe for?" "Not at all; I have
heard he resembles Abram Lincoln, and that
he is his half-brother." The driver then became satisfied and talkative. He stated he
had heard the story frequently, and was a
relative of the Enloe family himself.

Passing Yellow Hill, the Indian school sup-
ported by the government, a down-grade of
three or four miles brought us to a beautiful,
rich valley farm, the present home of Wesley,
and the old Abraham Enloe homestead. The
house was not unlike many of the old houses
in North Carolina—one story, the roof sloping
down over the piazza, with the company-room
opening on the porch. Mr. Enloe and his
wife were seated in front, a picture of undis-
turbed contentment and rural happiness.

MRS. JULIA ENLOE BIRD.

Daughter of Wesley Enloe and therefore Niece of
Abraham Lincoln.

The driver carried his team to the barn, and Mrs. Enloe retired to look after the dinner.

Mr. Enloe was about six feet, two or three inches tall, and, to my great disappointment, bald-headed; his right shoulder a little lower than his left; when standing, just slightly stooped forward. Our conversation took a varied turn—the force bill, the Alliance, crops, walnut rails, etc. I inquired finally if he had a picture of himself before he lost his hair. His daughter Julia, about nineteen years old, was summoned and brought a basketful of photographs. My attention was taken at once by the striking resemblance between Julia and Abraham Lincoln. The picture with a full head of hair failed to satisfy me of a striking face resemblance between Wesley Enloe and Abraham Lincoln. The photograph was taken the year Lincoln was killed, in Waynesville, to which place Mr. Enloe had carried a drove of beef-cattle the summer of 1865.

Mr. Enloe stated that he had never heard his father's name mentioned in his family in connection with Abraham Lincoln. He said: "I was the youngest of a family of sixteen. Such might have been the fact, but of course the older ones would not be apt to talk to me on a subject like that to which you allude. About 1871, say ten years ago, I learned and heard the story read from an Asheville paper for the first time."

The subject was dropped until four, when I started for home. I remarked, after thanking him for his hospitality, that I was perhaps the only man who had ever called just to look at him. The old man was without his coat, with wool hat, narrow brim. He replied pleasantly: "Now that you have seen me, what do you think?" My reply was that I must confess that I was disappointed, but that now seeing him with his hat on, with his hands crossed behind him (a favorite posture with Mr. Lincoln), taking in the whole six feet, three or four inches, there was a resemblance which I had no doubt was greater twenty-five years past. The resemblance in the case of Miss Julia is striking.

The old gentleman then related the following incident: "Two months past, in Dillsboro, in my daughter's parlor (she married in that town) is a map picture of President Lincoln. She said to me, 'Look at that picture. Did you ever see a better picture of my brother Frank?' Frank is my son and I have always heard he was much like my brother Scroup, who was said to be very like his father Abraham Enloe. I favor my mother's people. In size I am like the Enloes."

I failed to find Frank Enloe at home. At Dillsboro, having a draft to cash, I was informed by the hotel-keeper that William Enloe would cash it. On going into the store, filled with customers, I recognized William Enloe by his resemblance to Mr. Lincoln.

On my return east, arriving at Asheville at 3 P.M., I had dismissed the subject from my mind, but resolved to see Colonel Davidson, the father of our late attorney-general. I found him at home, willing to talk. And now, Mr. Editor, here is Colonel Davidson's story as your correspondent remembers it :

"Abram Enloe lived in Rutherford county. He had in his family a girl named Nancy Hanks, about ten or twelve years of age. He moved from Rutherford to Buncombe and settled on a branch of the Ocona, in what was afterwards Haywood, and what is now Swain county. At the end of eight years he moved to the house at the foot of the Smoky mountain, the place above described as the present home of Wesley Enloe.

"Soon after Abram moved his own daughter, Nancy Enloe, against his wish, ran away and married a Kentucky gentleman named Thompson, from Hardin county in that State.

"In the meantime during the absence of Mrs. Nancy Enloe Thompson in Kentucky, at the home of Abram Enloe a son was born to Nancy

Hanks, then about twenty or twenty-one years
of age. The relations between Mrs. Enloe and
her husband became, as a matter of course,.
unpleasant.

"There is a lady now living," says Colonel
Davidson, " who, as a girl, was visiting Abram
Enloe. This lady says that Nancy Enloe
Thompson, having become reconciled with her
parents, had returned from Kentucky to North
Carolina. They were to start to Kentucky
again in a few days, and she remembered hear-
ing a neighbor say, 'I am glad Nancy Hanks and
her boy are going to Kentucky with Mrs.
Thompson. Mrs. Enloe will be happy again.'

" I married into the Enloe family myself. I
settled Abram Enloe's estate, and have frequently heard this tradition during my life,
and have no doubt of its truth."

He added the following story, which is significant :

" I am a lawyer. I was seated in my office,.
since the war and soon after its close. A gen-

tleman called, introduced himself as Thompson
and stated he learned that I was the man who
settled Abram Enloe's estate; that he was a
a son of Nancy Enloe Thompson. He stated,
among other things, that he was a Democrat,
and had been an Indian agent during the Lincoln administration.

"I asked," said Col. Davidson, "how Lincoln, who was a Republican, appointed him, a
Democrat, an Indian agent?"

Thompson replied that Lincoln was under
some great obligation to his (Thompson's)
mother, and expressed a desire to aid her, if
possible, in some substantial way. She finally
consented that he might do something for her
son, and this is the way I got my appointment.

I have written this at your request, Mr. Editor, hoping that you will open your columns
to Col. Davidson and others, so that we may
follow the clues these people may furnish, and
thus see if there is any truth in this interesting North Carolina tradition.

STUDENT OF HISTORY.

On first blush there might seem to be a dis-
crepancy between the statement of Wesley
Enloe to the writer of these testimonies and
the above correspondent, but there is none.

He stated to the former that he had frequently heard the name Nancy Hanks spoken
by other and older members of the family in
his boyhood, but never heard his father mention the name or episode. He stated to the
latter that he had never heard Lincoln's name
associated with the name of his father or the
family; that he was the youngest of his
father's sixteen children, and they had, doubtless, kept the matter from him because (such
is the inference) of his juniority. I know that
Wesley Enloe has taken no serious thought of
the matter; that he is an extremely retired and
modest citizen, never, doubtless, having had a
biography of Lincoln in his house, and the incidents herein related came to him by degrees,
dawned on him gradually like so many reve-
lations. It must be remembered that he was

born two years, according to history, and perhaps four or five years according to the North Carolina tradition by some of the witnesses, after the birth of Mr. Lincoln. The fact was recalled by the older and knowing ones, by the association of the name Nancy Hanks with that of the great emancipator, and the statements of those who had been so fortunate as to obtain admissions from Mr. Lincoln himself, his mother and their Kentucky neighbors. Again it must be borne in mind that the Enloes were citizens of the same neighborhood and doubtless friends of Mr. Lincoln's from the very beginning of his public career.

The episode was a matter of extraordinary local notoriety in the most secret way, for the reason, as explained by many of the old people who were familiar with it, that Abraham Enloe was a very prominent citizen and greatly respected and admired by his neighbors and fellow-citizens, and the head of one of the best families of North Carolina, as well as through genuine sympathy for Nancy Hanks, who, according to the tradition, was held in unaffected esteem by the settlement.

It is interesting to note that the *Observer* correspondent is one of the very few intelligent students of Wesley Enloe who, even at his advanced age, when his features are pinched and sharpened by years and toil, fails to see in him a striking facial as well as bodily resemblance to Abraham Lincoln.

C. A. RAGLAND, ESQ.

Mr. Ragland is a citizen of Missouri and a leading attorney of the town of Stockton. He wrote:

"In reply to your letter to my wife have to say: About twelve years ago I called on Col. T. G. C. Davis at his office in St. Louis, Mo. At that time I lived in Illinois. Col. Davis was a relative of mine, his mother having been a Miss Ragland of Kentucky. Col. Davis was also born in Kentucky, and was a cousin of Jeff Davis, President of the Confederacy.

"Col. Davis having once resided for a long while in Illinois, the conversation naturally turned upon her times and men. He said he was personally and intimately acquainted with President Lincoln—was often associated with him, as well as against him, in law cases before the Supreme Court of Illinois; that they, as members of a committee of the Constitutional Convention (I think of 1844 or 5) of Illinois, drafted the most of the Constitution. He said that he knew the mother of Lincoln; that he was raised in the same neighborhood in Kentucky, and that it was generally understood, without question, in that neighborhood, that Lincoln, the man that married the President's mother, was not the father of the President, but that his father's name was Enloe.

"These facts I have a distinct recollection of. Col. Davis died about three years ago, in Denton, Texas."

COL. JOHN D. CAMERON.

Col. Cameron was a native of North Carolina. He graduated with honor from the University, and was a man of deep and varied learning and spotless reputation. He was a professional journalist; was many years editor of the Asheville *Citizen*, a bright daily. He was the author of the "North Carolina Handbook." The congenial colonel, at a ripe age, has recently passed away. He wrote:

"I am glad you have undertaken the 'Lincoln Mystery,' if such it can be styled, for you are on the spot, in the center of authority, and with the aid and cooperation of the relatives of the distinguished subject of the memoir. I believe all that I have heard. Col. A. T. Davidson is my reliable informant. I wish you success in your enterprise."

As some of the foregoing witnesses have referred to Hon. Wm. H. Thomas and Col. Allen T. Davidson, we deem it proper to briefly tell who they are.

Col. Thomas was born in Buncombe county, in a few miles of the scene of the event herein

recorded, about the year 1806. He was bereft of his father at an early age. He studied
grammar between the plow-handles, looking
at his book at the end of each row. He
acquired large real estate possessions, and by
the time he reached manhood he amassed a
fortune. He got into the good graces of the
Cherokee chief, Yonaguskah; was baptized by
the old chief as his son and made his successor.

He lived four years in Washington and
read the law of nations under John C. Calhoun.
He represented his section in both branches
of the State legislature. He was one of the
most distinguished men of the State in his day.

Col. Allen T. Davidson is an aged and retired lawyer residing in Asheville. In the
prime of life he was one of the ablest criminal
lawyers in the State. He is the father of ex-
Attorney-General Theo. F. Davidson. He
enjoyed a most intimate acquaintance with
the people who are the custodians of the Lincoln tradition, and understood it substantially
as herein revealed.

COL. WM. H. THOMAS.

Orator, Politician and Financier—a Brilliant and Versatile Genius. Father-in-law of Hon. A. C. Avery,
ex-Associate Justice of the Supreme Court. A Con-
temporary of Abraham Lincoln. He was a custodian
of and a believer in the Lincoln-Enloe Tradition.

CHAPTER II.

A COMPARATIVE STUDY.

The writer has been careful to accept the statements of none but persons of the highest character relative to the North Carolina tradition.

As the written or historical account of Lincoln's origin is nothing more nor less than tradition transferred to the printed page, we direct the reader to the most authentic personal biography of Mr. Lincoln in existence— that of Herndon and Weik—the former gentleman having been associated with Mr. Lincoln in the practice of the law for more than a quarter of a century. In various instances Mr. Herndon admits that Mr. Lincoln's origin, so far as he had been able to trace it, was enveloped in gloom. He even admits that in his intimate lifetime association with Mr.

Lincoln he never knew him to refer to his ancestry in his hearing but once, and that Mr. Lincoln was always painfully reticent on the subject.

Mr. Herndon does, however, go so far as to say that Mr. Lincoln divulged some fact with reference to his ancestry to a Chicago journalist by the name of Scripps, but at the same time, enjoined secrecy, and that Mr. Scripps died years ago without revealing it to any one. All that Mr. Lincoln ever said to Mr. Herndon was a few words about his maternity. Averring that Mr. Lincoln's origin and ancestry were doubtful, if not unknown, in one breath, Mr. Herndon, in the next breath, traces his origin and ancestry on either side to the third generation. This is mysterious, and can only be accounted for by the fact that the biographer was conscious that he had failed to find the real source of his illustrious subject, and his innate honesty sought ventilation in these frequent admissions.

In fact, after reading Mr. Herndon's ac-
·count of Mr. Lincoln's origin, so strong and
·recurring are the insinuations in that direction,
·that one is lead ·to think that Mr. Herndon
·himself knew that Thomas Lincoln was not
·the actual father of Abraham Lincoln.
Whether Mr. Herndon knew who Lincoln's
real father was, it does not concern us to say,
·further than that we believe he did not, and,
·therefore, acting the part of a close personal
·friend of Mr. Lincoln and his family, and at
·the same time endeavoring to be a true biog-
·rapher, he recorded Thomas Lincoln, the re-
·puted father of Abraham Lincoln, as his
·father, coupling with the record the sugges-
·tion that the public are entitled to the benefit
·of a grave doubt as to its truthfulness.

In Mr. Herndon's story, or, as we shall here-
·after style it, the Kentucky tradition, there is
·presumptive evidence that Mr. Lincoln knew
·who his father was. In the North Carolina
·tradition there is direct and positive evidence

that he knew who his father was. In the
Kentucky tradition there is no positive evidence that he ever revealed who his father
was. In the North Carolina tradition there is
positive evidence that he did reveal who his
father was.

The question naturally arises with the person who is not thoroughly familiar with Mr.
Lincoln's character, "Why did he withhold
from the world the truth of who his father
was? And if, in any case he imparted this
knowledge, why was he choice in his reposi-
tory of the same? Why did he charge one
person with temporary secrecy, as is intimated
in the case of Scripps, and to another person
accompany his divulgence with no restrictions,
as is plainly shown in the case of Davis?
Why did he open this secret of his ancestry to
comparative strangers and withhold it from his
law-partner and close friend?"

Our answer to the first question is, that before Abraham Lincoln entered public life he

ABRAHAM LINCOLN.

Comparative likenesses of Lincoln and Enloe, according
to this narrative half-brothers, arranged here to facili-
tate the study of family resemblance as an argument
for the contention of this book.

WESLEY M. ENLOE, Age 81.

was shut up in the wilderness of obscurity;
there was no occasion for the world to know
who his ancestors were ; but when he came before the public as a leader, he very rapidly de-
veloped into an adroit politician whose ambition was boundless, and he sought encourage-
ment and support beyond partizan lines ; therefore, one of the probable reasons why he maintained so studious a silence on the question
of his origin might have been the politic one.

In answer to the second question, Abraham
Lincoln was a man of the nicest discriminat-
ing sense, and he never lost an opportunity to
use this rare endowment to promote, in an
honorable way, his personal interest. He was
the candidate of the anti-slavery party for president. He told Mr. Scripps, the official representative of a great anti-slavery journal, personally, who his father was, but forbade further publication of the matter, because his sagacity suggested, for reasons that are obvious,
that silence, in that quarter, would be golden.

He explained to Mr. Davis, who was not a newspaper correspondent nor a politician, but a plain citizen and voter, on the eve of the latter's visit to his old home in North Carolina, that he was of southern extraction; that his right name was Enloe, but that he had always gone by the name of his stepfather. Davis was going to the south; to a democratic, proslavery State, to the home of Mr. Lincoln's traditional ancestors, and the shrewd presidential candidate knew that a little proud though quiet reminder by Davis at the distant south could not possibly impair his prospects for success.

In answer to the last question, Mr. Lincoln withheld himself, as to his origin, from Mr. Herndon, doubtless for the same reason that he refused to invest one of his greatest generals with an important mission on a certain occasion.

This seeming incongruousness of character and conduct in Mr. Lincoln was one of his marked individualities. This will be better understood, and we are quite certain the reader's credence will be strengthened in the probability of Mr. Lincoln's exercising this characteristic on certain occasions, when it is learned what a very distinguished authority has said of this very phase of Mr. Lincoln's character. The reader may then see how easy it was for him to reveal who his father was to Scripps and Davis and not even to Herndon or any one else so far as is known.

We quote from the biography of Lincoln by the great and learned Dr. Holland:

"The fact was that he rarely showed more than one aspect of himself to one man. He opened himself to men in different directions."

The Kentucky tradition has it that Thomas Lincoln was married to Nancy Hanks in 1806. The North Carolina tradition says that Nancy Hanks lived in the home of Abraham Enloe in the early part of the century—one witness says about the year 1805; another says from about 1803 to 1808. The traditional testimony establishes the fact that it was at the dawn of the century.

Mr. Herndon produces the Lincoln family record purporting to have been taken originally from the Lincoln family Bible. It shows to have been badly mutilated. The record has much the appearance of having been written consecutively and at one sitting. It is in the even handwriting of Mr. Lincoln's mature, professional years. It is, therefore, unknown how and when these dates, twenty-one in all, covering a period of sixty-three years, were furnished. A plausible way of accounting for this record may be seen in this simple surmise :

Some time in the early fifties, certainly after the death of Mr. Lincoln's reputed father, for the latter event is recorded among the last in the same handwriting, out of respect for the people with whom he had come up, Mr. Lincoln paid a visit to his step-

mother's, in Coles county, and stepping into a
bookstore on leaving Springfield, he purchased
a family Bible, containing a place for a record,
with which to present his old stepmother, for
whom it is said he entertained a tender feeling. This indeed would have been a very
appropriate and touching memento of the
occasion of his first visit after his reputed
father's death. Then it was that the family
record, as reproduced by Mr. Herndon, was
penned down by Mr. Lincoln from his own
memory aided by that of his stepmother. A
most striking evidence of the probable cor-
rectness of this surmise may be seen in the
completeness of the record of the members of
the family of his stepmother and the marked
incompleteness of the records of Thomas
Lincoln, Nancy Hanks, and Mr. Lincoln's
alleged full sister. The birth of neither
Thomas Lincoln nor Nancy Hanks is recorded. Why the birth of Mr. Lincoln's
mother is left out is a mystery when, accord-

ing to Mr. Herndon, it must have been well known. He gives her age, at the time of her marriage to Thomas Lincoln, as twenty-three.

Again the Kentucky tradition has it that there was a daughter born to Thomas and Nancy Lincoln in 1807, before Abraham, whom it records as first seeing the light 12th February, 1809. But there is a serious dis--crepancy here which Mr. Lincoln's biographers have not been able to reconcile.

Nicolay and Hay, the latter our late ambas-sador to England and present Secretary of State, both of whom were very intimate with Mr. Lincoln, say that this sister's name was Nancy and contend that such was her real name. Mr. Herndon contends persist--ently that her name was Sarah and that the family knew her by that name. Her name appears of record in the family Bible as Nancy. Mr. Herndon surmises that the record was torn away down to the word Nancy and that the name was intended for that of

the President's mother. There is no evidence
that Mr. Lincoln ever paid any attention to
this alleged sister. There was another Sarah
in the family, daughter of Thomas Lincoln's
second wife by her first husband. Mr. Lincoln's alleged full sister is said not to have
resembled him in stature, being short and
thick-set.

It is hard to imagine such stolid indifference and cold neglect on the part of such a
man as Abraham Lincoln for an only sister—
the nearest relative he had in the world. But
such is the statement of his biographer. She
was only two years his senior. At an early
age Lincoln began to dream of his future; as
he grew older it seems that he would certainly
become interested in this sister, and like Webster who helped to educate his brother, and
Davy Crockett who worked off his father's
debts, have striven to bring her up to a
position of respectability in society equal with
the best of her class; if he had failed in

this ambition, and, as his biographer intimates, this failure had been followed by her misfortune, it had impressed the world more favorably and deeply if his historian had said something like this: "Throughout her brief though sad career, from childhood to the grave, this only sister of Abraham Lincoln was followed by him, through evil as well as good report, with unremitting interest and tender solicitude."

It was not in Abraham Lincoln's humane, manly heart to have been even careless of the welfare of an only sister. To this, as to his own origin as detailed by his biographer, there is attached a mystery. Lincoln, young though he was when his melancholy mother died, was wise—he had been lead, doubtless by none other person save Nancy Hanks, through these dim paths into the light.

A thorough examination of the Bible record, and the biography by Herndon alongside that by Nicolay and Hay, shows plainly that there

A. LINCOLN.

TRADITIONAL SON OF ABRAM ENLOE.

For the further development of this comparative
study.

WESLEY ENLOE

AT THE AGE OF 81. SON OF ABRAHAM ENLOE.

The most striking similarity between Mr. Lincoln and Wesley Enloe is their physical formation and characteristics, which may be seen from the above comparative standing likeness.

is something mysterious and inexplicable in connection with this alleged sister.

A painstaking comparison of the North Carolina and Kentucky traditions will show but little discord relative to the probable date of Mr. Lincoln's birth and that of the marriage of Nancy Hanks and Thomas Lincoln. The North Carolina tradition does not pretend to fix the date of Nancy Hanks's leaving Abraham Enloe's. It is no more definite than the early, very early, years of the century. Some of the witnesses do go so far as to say that Abraham Enloe came from Rutherford to Buncombe about the year 1805, and that Nancy Hanks came with him.

There is no conflict here as to the birth of Mr. Lincoln or the marriage of his mother, for Abraham Enloe's coming to Western North Carolina might have been a few years earlier, as another competent witness says about 1803. Mr. Herndon says the Washington county, Kentucky, records show that the marriage took place in 1806.

Passing the alleged birth of the whole (?) sister as too mysterious to admit of human intermeddling, except to invite the reader to investigate for himself, we pass·to the advent of our illustrious subject. The family record has it that Abraham Lincoln was born February 12, 1809.

It is a fact of history that, at the time of the marriage of Thomas Lincoln to Nancy Hanks the former could neither read nor write, and while it is intimated that the latter could do both, it is extremely doubtful. Every whit of history and tradition in regard to this particular personage is agreed that she was, almost from her infancy, without any one who would have cared a fig whether she learned the alphabet. Moreover, it would have been the most natural thing in the world for Nancy Hanks to drift along in the woods without a thought of beginning a family record, even if she could have written, until after the lapse of more than a decade, perhaps, and the quarrels

between Thomas Lincoln and the Enloes,
as our tradition testifies, coupled with the ever-
present reminder of the name, engendered in
the heart of Thomas Lincoln a lasting hatred.
One might guess, and hit it, that the record
which should have read February 12th, 1806,
was made to read February 12th, 1809. Let
this be as it may, there is no question as to the
fact that this family record of Abraham Lincoln's birth is pure matter of tradition. There
is no evidence that it was ever made matter of
record in the family of Lincoln's reputed parents
until 1851, and then the only chance to get it
done was for Lincoln to do it himself. Verily,
who can say that Abraham Lincoln was not
the architect of his own fortune?

If one should say that, after reading the
accounts of the utter barrenness and misery of
Thomas Lincoln's home, for such is the record,
and the perfect worthlessness of Thomas
himself, one could not imagine such things as
pencil and paper, far less pen and ink and

family record, placed there by Thomas's hands, or at his behest, there need be no cause for surprise. Indeed, if the historical account of Thomas Lincoln, the reputed father of the great president, be true, it is exceedingly uncertain whether he worried over so small a thing as the advent of a child into the world, particularly if it were not his child. It is equally doubtful whether the poor, sad-hearted Nancy Hanks, brooding her life away in the thick gloom of a dirty hovel, ever entertained so delightful a fancy as that of possessing a family record.

Mr. Lincoln himself, according to his biographers, accepted the 12th February, 1809, as the time of his coming into the world. But in this Abraham Lincoln, no doubt, found himself in a place somewhat like that in which Zeb Vance once discovered himself.

Vance was a candidate for the legislature from Buncombe and his competitor, who was much his senior, objected, among other points,

MISS ELIZA ENLOE.

Daughter of Wesley M. Enloe, and Traditional Niece of
Abraham Lincoln.

to Vance's youthfulness. In his reply Zeb, in a very apologetic air, united with the most affected urbanity of manner, said: "Fellow citizens, I would cheerfully have been born earlier, if it had been in my power, but my father and mother gave me no earthly chance about the matter. I humbly beg pardon, therefore, and will try and do better next time." Mr. Lincoln knew very little more about this event of his life than did Zeb Vance about the similar event of his.

Passing a great number of expressions in Mr. Lincoln's biography by Messrs. Herndon and Weik, we come to another which we cannot forbear to notice in this running comparative review of the North Carolina and Kentucky traditions.

Mr. Herndon says he called upon Mr. Lincoln's stepmother after the death of Thomas Lincoln and the assassination of the president. The express purpose of his visit was to obtain data for his prospective biography of Mr. Lincoln. Of course the very first thing he did

was to endeavor to find out all he could about
Mr. Lincoln's parents. This old lady was
very communicative until Mr. Herndon came
to Nancy Hanks, the president's mother, and
her predecessor in the Lincoln household, and
here she was mournfully mum. What was
there associated with the inoffensive name of
Nancy that caused this old lady to exercise
such significant reticence? We say inoffensive
name, because the president's mother had been
dead forty-six years, and could not come near
the second Mrs. Lincoln. Could it possibly
have been a false sense of virtue or a deeply
respectful regard for Abraham Lincoln, or
something less exemplary in this old lady that
caused her to withold her knowledge of Nancy
Hanks which was undoubtedly extensive and
valuable, from Lincoln's historian? Could it
have been that this successor of Nancy
Hanks, who, in her early life, had lived in
the same neighborhood in Kentucky in which
it occurred, and who, before that, had been Tom
Lincoln's sweetheart, was perfectly familiar

with the event herein related by three generations of as good people as North Carolina
affords? What was there about Nancy
Hanks's life that she needs must decline to talk
about or to impart to one who is entitled to all
the facts? Here is another unsolved and
unsolvable mystery, should it devolve upon the
Kentucky tradition to do the solving. We
leave it to the reader to say whether the North
Carolina tradition furnishes the key to it.

The Kentucky tradition verifies ours when
it says that at a very early age Nancy Hanks
was taken from her mother and sent to live
with some of her worthless relatives. Nancy
Hanks herself, according to the biographer,
was a spurious child, and doubtless never
saw her father, and, being forced from her
mother at a very early age, virtually became
an orphan. The North Carolina tradition says
she was an orphan girl. In the face of this
fact one can see how probable it is that Nancy
Hanks, at a very tender age for one of her sex,

rambled into the world, and just as she was passing into young womanhood made her way to North Carolina and at last into the home of Abraham Enloe.

Was there any particular and plausible reason why she should have drifted toward North Carolina and the house of Abraham Enloe? At that early time there was a steady stream of emigrants, travelers, horse-drovers and visitors flowing back and forth between Western North Carolina and Kentucky. It was an easy thing for a person to obtain company and means of transportation, by watching the chances, from one of these sections to the other. The special reason why Nancy Hanks might have made Abraham Enloe's home, in particular, her destination might have been the fact that members of the Enloe family lived at that time in Kentucky, and in her immediate circle of acquaintance.

Realizing that she was alone in the world, Nancy Hanks decided to seek a new home

ROBERT WALKER ENLOE.

Son of Wesley Enloe and Traditional Nephew of Abraham Lincoln. Compare this likeness with the Frontispiece in Herndon's Lincoln, 2d Vol.

among strangers away from the touch of her worthless relatives, and begin the battle of life anew and on her own responsibility. Making known her resolve to some of the Kentucky Enloes, or having it suggested to her by some of them, she was accordingly directed to the Kentucky Enloes' North Carolina kinsman; and seeking and availing herself of the first opportunity, Nancy put her resolution into effect, and soon found herself in the respectable and happy home of Abraham Enloe, of Rutherford first and afterward Buncombe county, North Carolina. That she lived in his Buncombe home there is not the shadow of doubt.

That the Enloes lived among the Hankses and Lincolns in Kentucky, both traditions are agreed and positive.

According to the biographical description, Abraham Lincoln did no more resemble Thomas Lincoln, his reputed father, than did the rankest stranger, either physically or intellectually. The only prominent character-

istics which he inherited from Nancy Hanks
were his slender form and melancholy temper-
ament. This melancholy itself in Lincoln
and his mother may be accounted for in the
unhappy step the latter was lead to take in the
Carolina mountains.

We recommend to the reader a serious parallel study of these two traditions. The subject
of Mr. Lincoln's paternal origin has engaged
the time and attention of some of the most distinguished men of our country, and, in every
instance the result of their investigations,
owing to their never having gotten hold of the
true thread of his beginning, has only been to
elicit increased wonder and speculation—wonder because of the seemingly impenetrable
mystery that settled about so tall a figure in
our history. Even Jesus of Nazareth, the
world's example of lowliness, had the authority of heaven for his paternal origin and an intelligent carpenter for his earthly ward, but if
we are to accept the story of Lincoln's pater-

nal ancestor, as told by his biographers, *he* had neither.

But if we shall believe the disinterested accounts of as honorable and trustworthy citizens as North Carolina contains, handed down to them by as good men and women as the early half of the nineteenth century produced, some of the mist will hereafter not hover around the true paternal origin of Abraham Lincoln, and there will be opened a new and sunnier avenue in which the honest and generous student of American history's most remarkable man may confidently walk.

CHAPTER III.

ABE LINCOLN'S HALF-BROTHER.

Wesley M. Enloe is now eighty-seven years of age. He is six feet high. When he was in the prime of life he was taller. His build is slender with the appearance of toughness and sineviness. His shoulders are narrow and somewhat rounded at the points. He is thin from chest to back. He stands almost erect, and his head, when standing or sitting, assumes an attitude indicative of firmness and decision. His hands and fingers are large and long, and his arms and legs are long and skeleton-looking. His legs, in length, are out of proportion to his body. His neck is long; face lean; forehead high and slightly sloping; his nose is large and straight and his mouth is prominent—the underlip large and protruding. His head will require about a number seven and one-eighth hat. His walk and various body posturings are inimitable. We shall desist from entering into a description of them for the simple reason that one who is familiar with Abraham Lincoln will say that we have purloined his physical idiosyncrasies. The truth is that the two men are so much alike that one hesitates to presume upon the much-abused credulity of mankind by a faithful portrayal of the personal and bodily characteristics of Wesley Enloe, where Mr. Lincoln is well known, and feels constrained to cry out, with Philip of old: "Come and see."

His address is plain, extremely unassuming and deferential, and one is soon at ease in his company. He has lived his whole life at the old homestead. He is well known over his own and adjoining counties. His character is beyond reproach, and it makes the western hillside of his life sunny and serene. He has always been an influential, well-to-do farmer, whose judgment has safely been deferred to by his neighbors in matters of common sense.

The cuts of him here presented were made from poor kodaks, taken when he was eighty-one and eighty-eight years of age, after, by course of nature, he had lost much of his manly vigor. There was no other likeness of him in existence. A cut made from a good photograph, or from a portrait when he was fifty, would have answered the purpose of its appearing here more satisfactorily and fairly.

We asked Messrs. D. Appleton & Company, who are now in possession of Herndon's Lincoln, to kindly allow us to use the frontispiece of their first volume as a comparative likeness with that of Wesley Enloe, but they courteously declined to comply with our request. The likeness of Mr. Lincoln here referred to presents him clean shaven, and would have served our purpose of comparison better than any representation of him of which we have any knowledge. But with what we have it will not require an expert to detect the striking resemblance.

We also asked Messrs. Appleton & Co. to allow us to use a few passages from Herndon & Weik's biography on condition of credit to the book, but they respectfully declined in this also. We have therefore been studiously careful not to quote a single one of that biography's misgivings (for such is one's feeling as he reads it) as to whether Mr. Lincoln really had a paternal ancestor.

We have, however, briefly compared the misty, winterish chapter of that book on Mr. Lincoln's origin with our tradition, from what we had assimilated by reading it. We recommend to the reader who desires seriously to inquire into our tradition, as well as to study judiciously the life of a truly great one among many of earth's so-called great men, the biography of Abraham Lincoln by Messrs. Herndon & Weik.

But to recur to the subject of personal resemblance: We shall ask that the personal experience of one out of scores of similar experiences may suffice to convey to you some idea of the remarkable physical likeness which Wesley M. Enloe bears to Abraham Lincoln, and the force with which it strikes even a casual observer:

"In 1894 Mr. Theodore Harris, of San Antonio, Texas, a cultured gentleman, was stopping in my town. He had heard the Lincoln tradition, and was thoroughly acquainted with the personal characteristics of Abraham Lincoln. Mr. Harris and myself made a trip up the Ocona Lufta river on a fishing and hunting expedition. Passing up the river, as we were nearing Mr. Wesley Enloe's place, we saw a man coming on foot down the road toward us. Before we were quite near enough to discern his features, Mr. Harris, in an animated but half-suppressed manner, pointed in the direction of the man and said: 'That is Mr. Enloe of whom I have heard—the alleged half-brother of Lincoln,' or words to that effect. Sure enough, on coming up to him, we found that it was Wesley Enloe, for I had met him before. I confessed to Mr. Harris that I had never before witnessed so remarkable an incident. He explained to me, as well as I can now recall his words, that 'the personal resemblance of Wesley Enloe to Abraham Lincoln flashed upon him like a revelation.'"

SION T. EARLY.

Dillsboro, N. C., Jan. 9, 1899.

Mr. Early is an intelligent gentleman of unquestioned veracity. Mr. Harris lives in San Antonio, Texas.

A RECAPITULATION.

I am aware that in the heading of this chapter I have made a seemingly bold venture. The "half-brother" is not the son of Nancy Hanks by her second husband, for she was not married twice; he is not the son of Thomas Lincoln by his second wife, for his name is Enloe; his native State is North Carolina and not Kentucky. How, then, can he be Lincoln's half-brother? Only in this way: A native of North Carolina is the father of Abraham Lincoln, and not Thomas Lincoln, of Kentucky. Have I slandered the great Lincoln? Have I slandered the nation? Let the facts speak :

First.—The tradition exists; you have read the evidence in the foregoing chapter.

Second.—The silence of history. Search his biographies and you are convinced. Do not depend on isolated paragraphs from school histories not written in Kentucky nor Illinois. Why this silence?

Third.—A striking physical resemblance of the "half-brother" to Mr. Lincoln. I say "striking," because it has overcome high Lincolnian prejudice and forced conviction.

I shall give the experience of a gentleman, thoroughly trustworthy and competent, substantially as he gave it to me. It has the greater weight because it comes from a gentleman who, from my conference with him, I found wished the mist cleared away from Mr. Lincoln's paternity.

I cannot give his exact words and have not obtained permission to give his name; and so presume upon the reader's confidence in my veracity. However, I will here engage that if I am challenged I will promptly call on the gentleman in question to speak for himself.

He said he visited the home of Wesley Enloe, and spent the night. As was his wont he made a study of the former's physiognomy, though he had no case to make out. He said that Mr. Enloe did not suggest Lincoln. On returning to his home he was examining a description of a statue of Lincoln in one of the leading magazines, and paused to study the representation—it suggested Wes'ey Enloe, and the resemblance carried conviction. On inquiring more carefully into the tradition, his conviction was confirmed.

You say he would not have detected the resemblance if he had not first heard the tradition. But detecting the resemblance is different from being convicted by it. The observer was loath to believe the fact the resemblance proved.

The skeptic will further object that the resemblance is simply a coincidence. But the uniqueness of the coincidence is his misfortune. It is a coincidence on one side of which is a tradition authenticated by the most valid testimony, and on the other side the most re-

markable silence of history; a silence incred-
ible if the tradition is apocryphal, for no other
voice has ever been heard.   One note of history
would drown the alleged slander; but it has
not been heard.

Are the tradition and the silence a coincidence?

It cannot be said that this physical resemblance was the beginning of the tradition, for
the tradition existed before it was known, according to the testimony.

It cannot be said that the story causes men
to imagine there is a resemblance; skeptics
do not possess imaginations of such conveni-
ence.   The country is full of close observers
whose judgment cannot be affected by an idle
story, whatever their prejudice may be.

Fourth.—Clear, positive testimony.   I need
not recite the evidence bearing on the fact that
a young woman named Nancy Hanks was the
mother of an illegitimate child by Abraham
Enloe, and that she was conveyed to Kentucky,

either before or shortly after the birth of the child; you read the evidence in Chapter I.

If the evidence stopped here I should not feel myself vindicated against the charge of slander.

There might have been another Nancy Hanks.

But take the testimony of Mr. Joe Collins of Clyde, N. C., a man of unquestioned veracity; it runs as follows: He was in Texas; Judge Gilmore told him that he was raised in the community of Nancy Hanks, and she had a boy named Abraham. She married Tom Lincoln, a whisky distiller, and the boy took his name. He was about six years older than Abraham, but went to school with him, and he was the brightest boy in the community.

Now this testimony, saying nothing of the rest, must be gotten out of the way before I am a slanderer.

No one can reasonably doubt that Mr. Collins received these statements from a man who

represented himself to him as Judge Gilmore.
Now it devolves upon my prosecutor to do one
of the following things :

First, to prove that no such man as Judge
Gilmore spent his boyhood in the community
with young Lincoln and his mother, and that
Mr. Collins has been deceived. Establish it
in this way. Go, or send a representative to
the community, and let the most diligent and
general inquiry be made, and if nobody remembers a boy in that section (unless all the
old people are dead, or gone from there, who
remember young Lincoln) named Gilmore,
old enough to have been Lincoln's schoolmate,
and later left for Texas, or elsewhere, then we
give up that part of the testimony. Mr. Collins has been deceived. But if it is remembered that a boy named Gilmore grew up in
that community about the age of Lincoln, and
removed, the next thing to arrive at is that he
did not go to Texas, as far as the people know.
His kinsfolk can tell you, or some of the old

neighbors. If it is remembered that he lived
there at the time designated, and went to
Texas, the same people will know whether he
was a judge. If they do, the next thing to do
is to establish the fact that he was not reliable.
Few men reach the bench who are not reliable. The old people in the community of
his boyhood can give you his character there.
The people of the town in Texas where he
resided can tell you whether he was a man of
veracity. If he succeeds here Mr. Collins's
testimony is lost. If he fails the next thing
to do is to produce a second Nancy Hanks who
was married to a second Thomas Lincoln, and
who also had a boy named Abraham. If he
fails in one of these things I am vindicated:
if he succeeds in any one of them I am not convicted there is other testimony.

The positive character of the testimony in
North Carolina and the wide-spread and in-
eradicable conviction as to its truthfulness, and
the suspicious silence of biography put the

burden upon my prosecutor to make general, painstaking and impartial investigation on the scene of Lincoln's boyhood, and show that there is nothing in the "Nancy Hanks" story. Here he has the same disadvantages. This would seem to be my disadvantage, but it is his, in fact.

Kentucky naturally aspires to the honor of producing the great Lincoln; hence an insuperable reticence. The world will understand. But the retort may be made that in North Carolina the same aspiration, in some cases and the memory of the late unpleasantness in others, cause an undue readiness to ventilate the tradition. When you seek to obtain written statements you will find the retort of no great weight. It is too early for a Kentucky investigator to give in his experience. There is no readiness on the part of any one in North Carolina to ventilate the tradition.

The contention of some of Mr. Lincoln's

biographers is that, as we have noticed elsewhere, Thomas Lincoln and Nancy Hanks
had a daughter older than Abraham, and
that ends it. If this be so, there are two
Nancy Hankses. For Abraham Enloe had
some communication with one in Kentucky,
who had a child by him named Abraham.
It is a little unlikely that two women named
Nancy Hanks would each have a son named
Abraham, but it could have happened. Did
it happen? The existence of the Nancy with
a daughter older than her Abraham is *absolutely without proof.*

The record in the family Bible cannot be
relied on. One biographer thinks the oldest
daughter's name is mutilated. Some say her
name was one thing, some another. Lincoln
was utterly indifferent toward this sister.
Could she have been akin to him? Those
who persist in apotheosizing him had better
say no. There is positive proof that Thomas
Lincoln's second wife had a daughter named

Sarah. The record was not made till 1851, in Lincoln's own handwriting. He could not afford to distinguish between the two sets of children. Would he be likely to leave out of the record his stepmother's daughter by her first husband? There is doubt about the first "Nancy" having the daughter older than her Abraham. The absence of positive proof of the older daughter's existence and an unlikely coincidence jeopardize the existence of the first "Nancy."

But we know that the second "Nancy"—the North Carolina one—did exist and went to Kentucky under a cloud; had a son named Abraham.

Am I convicted? Not till the investigation is made, as above suggested, and none are found who know a fact which points clearly in the direction of Abraham Lincoln's illegitimate ancestry. As long as there remains a circumstance that suggests doubt, I am not convicted. It will be easier for the skeptic

to abuse than disabuse. If the testimony of
Mr. Joe Collins is not demolished and the
Kentucky investigator reports adversely,—and
I await results,—we have a case clear as
second-hand human evidence can make it.

Do Abraham Lincoln's historians tell the
truth when they aver that, after diligent search
where they were most likely to find, they are
unable to satisfy themselves or even to say
with assurance who Mr. Lincoln's father was?
Does any other State or locality in this country or elsewhere, lay claim to Lincoln's father
beside North Carolina? Does Kentucky herself lay serious claim to his paternal origin.
"Of what ancestry we know not," says Mr.
Watterson. Does North Carolina say who
Abraham Lincoln's father was? Are old,
distinguished citizens, for example Col. Davis
and Judge Gilmore, truthful? Are three generations of North Carolinians truthful? Is
the phenomenal physical likeness of Wesley
Enloe, Lincoln's traditional half-brother,

walking side by side with and, like a sturdy staff, supporting the North Carolina tradition, convincing and conclusive?

Reader, answer these questions, and say whether henceforth there is any doubt that Abraham Enloe, a strong, intelligent, leading North Carolina pioneer, was the great war president's father.

CHAPTER IV.

ABRAHAM ENLOE.

. Abraham Enloe, the traditional father of Abraham Lincoln, was the son of Gilbert Enloe, and was born in York district, South Carolina. The first of his American forebears came from Scotland about the middle of the seventeenth century. They landed first in Maryland, but subsequently moved to South Carolina, where they settled. They were school-teachers.

Abraham's father, being a man of more than ordinary mental endowment, the son received the rudiments of a good education. On coming of age he stepped from under his father's roof into the world to seek his fortune.

As a boy he was obedient and industrious and had made the most of his father's splendid tuition. He was, therefore, well equipped for one of his day for the struggle for life. He was of an excellent temper and judgment while yet a youth. He illustrated these in his choice of a country and clime in which to exercise his vigorous young faculties, as well as in the selection of a wife to share with him in their fruitions.

He sought a home first in Rutherford county, N. C., where he became acquainted with a Miss Egerton, a young lady of intellect and culture and a member of one of the best families in that section of the State. Their acquaintance at once ripened into genuine affection, and they were married and settled down to farming.

While a citizen of Rutherford county he established a reputation for uprightness of character which is still recalled with pride by his neighbors, and which followed him to his new home and throughout his life.

About the year 1803 or 1805, while early settlers were " staking their claims " further west, Abraham Enloe emigrated from Rutherford county and stopped on the Ocona Lufta, at the base of the Great Smoky mountains in Buncombe county.

In the settlement of his new home he encountered the usual difficulties of the pioneer. His granddaughter, a Mrs. Floyd, a bright and entertaining woman, said she remembered hearing her grandfather recount his experiences in coming to, and while trying to establish himself on, Ocona Lufta. The journey from Rutherford over great mountains and across dangerous streams was fraught with labor and peril. They were often compelled to improvise causeways for creeks and rivers, or to construct breastworks and dig wider the ways of the more primitive adventurer along the almost perpendicular mountain sides. When they had thus reached the summit of the high mountains, so steep was the descent, that they were obliged to tie good bits of trees to the rear ends of their wagons to prevent stampeding the teams. It was not infrequent that, because of the absence of any way save a deer or Indian trail, they packed their effects piecemeal on their backs over formidable mountains.

He was, however, fortunate in the choice of a stopping place. The Ocona Lufta is in the center of the highlands of the South, midway between the Hiawassa, Tennessee, and Nantahala on the one side, and the Tuckuseegih, French Broad and Swannanoa on the other.

It was a land to make the heart of the strong man grow stronger. The soil was rich. The trees were original. The air was pure, the water was crystal, and the forests were alive with a very great variety of birds and animals. It was a land whose star was not wormwood, but bright hope.

The only neighbors that were near to him after he had built his house were three families who had accompanied him from Rutherford, and the Cherokee Indians, in the heart of whose region he was.

There were other white families living within a distance of from twelve to fifty miles. A settlement in those days embraced a circuit of from twelve to fifteen miles, and was made up of as many families. It was such a settlement as this of which Abraham Enloe was the central figure and benefactor. In obedience to an ancient custom of mankind, each society or neighborhood, however small, must have its leading spirit and par-excellence adviser. Particularly must this needs be the practice of a community where the frequent hostilities of aboriginals, whose grievance is by no means imaginary, must be met. The common interest must be healthful and steadfast.

Abraham Enloe built his house in a fertile valley overlooking the Ocona Lufta, whose banks in summer are a continuous string of bouquets—Rhododendron, ivy and honeysuckle— to this day. It is an incident worthy of note, here, that this house is still standing, but slightly remodeled; and has been in four counties without being removed from its original foundations. It is a typical pioneer abode. One large log house with doors in either side directly opposite each other, and a chimney at one end built of natural boulders, with a remarkably wide fireplace.

A sure reminder of the brotherhood of the frontier community was the uniform nature of the settler's habitation. The style and value of the houses were as near the same as primitive ingenuity and limited resources could make them. No envy rose in the breast of the pioneer because of striking contrasts. The cabin did not droop and shiver in the shadow of the palace. Every man that crossed the settler's threshold crossed it like a knight.

Notwithstanding Abraham Enloe was generally absorbed in the more serious concerns of life, he found time for the then profitable diversion of hunting. The long-barreled flintlock was ever "picked and primed" for emergency use. The haunts of the deer, bear, and wild turkey were just outside his enclosure, and many are the thrilling stories of delightful sport in which he was always joined by some of his neighbors. On his broad doorstep and about the clean yard sat or slumbered long-eared deerhounds, watchful curs or surly mastiffs. Each of these bided patiently his call to dinner or duty, and all were indispensable in their respective spheres as followers of the chase, guards of the plantation and protectors of the home.

Returning once from the home of Hon. Felix Walker, whose place was west of the settlement a distance of fifty miles, Mrs. Enloe was amused to see her husband alight from his horse, across whose withers was a white bag, either end of which was strangely animate. Her wonder was turned to ridicule when she learned that the queer sack contained four fine deerhound puppies, the gift of the clever congressman. The pioneer would almost as readily have given up his rifle as his dogs. The keen solicitude which the settlers felt and manifested for these noble animals and the tender attachment which they in turn made known to their masters in their heroic rencounters with savage beasts and more savage men, appeal to our highest sensibilities. Their estimation was shared by men, women and children, and this, no doubt, helped to tie the Gordian knot of good neighborhood.

Abraham Enloe owned the best, and at first the only, horses in the neighborhood. He greatly valued these splendid animals, as well for their beauty as utility, and allowed nothing to go undone that would make them appear to the best advantage.

He was by profession a farmer, and early set a progressive pace for his neighbors in his chosen calling. He also possessed the only forge and blacksmith tools in the settlement, with which he kept in repair the farming implements of himself and neighbors.

There were no stores, and the nearest markets to which the settlement had access were Augusta, Ga., and Charleston, S. C. To these places, distant hundreds of miles, over the roughest of country and rudest of way, the settler hauled his produce or drove his live stock, which he eagerly exchanged for the necessities of civilized life.

Abraham Enloe possessed the only wagon in the settlement, and this served to transport, at one trip, the salt, powder and domestic consumed by the entire settlement a twelvemonth. Learning, on a certain occasion, that the settlement's meager supply of salt was exhausted, he harnessed his team, collected a few choice steers from his herd, and started for Augusta, Ga., where a fresh supply of this indispensable was procured, not only for himself, but for each of his neighbors.

He was a justice of the peace, an office of no little dignity in primitive times, and he was implicitly turned to as the final arbiter in adjusting differences between his neighbors. He was the trusted adviser of the politicians, great and small of his party, with whom he came in contact. The relations existing between himself and the Hon. Felix Walker, the first member of Congress from the Buncombe district, were the most cordial and intimate.

It was this same Felix Walker, a discreet leader of frontiersmen, who, while delivering himself of legislative responsibility, in a speech of some length in the House of Representatives, and observing what he construed to be an expression of weariness on the face of the Speaker and members, raised himself to his full height and assured them that he was aware of the fact that he had spoken at some length; that what he was saying might not interest them, but that it was his firm resolve to continue until he had done, and then, with reassured emphasis, he said: "Mr. Speaker, I wish the gentlemen of this House to understand that I am speaking for Buncombe!" Thus originated the phrase "speaking for Buncombe."

The house of Abraham Enloe was headquarters for the gospel. The pioneer preacher, no matter his creed, found there a warm welcome and partook of his hospitalities without the semblance of grudge.

Public worship was one of the strongest bonds of these early communities. At a period too early for the log church they came, for many miles, to the house of some prominent settler to an annual or semi-annual appointment of such men as brave old Cartwright or the brilliant Bascom. To them worship was not a mere diversion. ' It was a solemn responsibility and means of power that must be seriously regarded. Earnestness fitted them like a garment. They came to the place appointed for worship, if it was the mild season, in their shirt-sleeves, with their rifles on their shoulders. They were the synonym of simplicity, and every declaration based upon a straight interpretation of the Bible they accepted eagerly and without question.

With them there were few base coins; most
were ringing bright gold. From them have
sprung, like wheat from a virgin soil, the har-
vest of heroic men, whose mission it is to meet
and turn aside the wild, babbling stream of
innovation which now and then threatens to
mingle its noxious floods with the old abiding
river of human progress.

Abraham Enloe's house was often converted
into a settlement sanctuary. It was little more
than a half-dozen miles from his house to the
capital of the Cherokees. His policy toward
these children of the forest was benevolence—
the true neighbor; while white men of other
settlements often provoked a "hurrying to and
fro" upon the war-path, Abraham Enloe and
his dusky neighbors snugly reclined in the
bosom of peace.

Abraham Enloe was a man of great con-
servatism and judgment. There was no rash-
ness in his nature. He, therefore, sought,
among the first things after settling in West-

ern Carolina, to establish a permanent friendship between himself and the Chief and most
influential men of the Cherokees. He ever
enjoyed the respect and confidence of the band,
and his relations with the two chiefs, Yonaguskah and Sawinookih, were the most intimate and pleasant.

It was indeed fortunate for Abraham Enloe
and his neighbors that they were contemporaries of such dynasties as those of Yonaguskah and Sawinookih. These chiefs were both
men of great natural ability, especially Yonaguskah. He was pronounced by a competent
judge, who knew both well, the intellectual
peer of John C. Calhoun.

The following story, as told by Colonel
W. H. Thomas, who was an eye-witness, will
serve to illustrate the superstitious wisdom of
this old Chief : The Cherokees, like most men
of their race who come too near the blessed
influence of Caucasian civilization, became
addicted to strong drink. Yonaguskah, though

SAWINOOKIH.

The First Chief Cherokees, in His Old Age and in
Civilian Apparel.

himself an occasional victim of its subtle embraces, determined upon the prohibition of strong drink among his entire band. Suddenly he fell into a stupor. So deep and mysterious was his slumbers that the whole town heard of it. They came flocking to his side and looked long and sadly upon him and decided that he was dead. In agony they waited for the return of their venerable Chief to his senses and his wondrous walks and ways. But no sign of life appeared, and over a thousand of his faithful children determined, in deep sorrow, to celebrate their ancient and impressive rite of funeral and sepulture. Forming in single file they danced around the prostrate Chief, mumbling their weird death-chant.

Suddenly, in the midst of the solemn performance, Yonaguskah arose, and standing in their midst with the inspiration of a prophet and majesty of a king, told them that he had been translated to the "happy hunting-grounds," and that while there he had communed with the Great Spirit relative to their happiness. He said he was impressed that intemperance would be the means of their extermination, and advised them to turn their backs on the "fire-water" of the white man. He said he had served them for over forty years without asking for a cent of pay, and the only thing he exacted was their obedience. With profound feeling he bemoaned his own and his people's mistake, and concluded by directing Colonel Thomas to act as clerk and write the following: "The undersigned Cherokees, belonging to the town of Qualla, agree to abandon the use of spirituous liquors."

Gravely stepping forward the old Chief signed first and was then followed by the whole town. For many years this pledge was kept inviolate, and at last, when some yielded to the influence of the whites and were lead to break it, Yōnaguskah established the " whipping-post" and enforced his simple pledge with the rigor of an English statute in the reign of Henry the Eighth.

Sawinookih was a man of great native wit. In one of his visits, as Chief, to Washington he imbibed a little too prodigally of "fire-water," and wandering around in the bewildering glare of lights and city pageant (for it was in the night), he became "lost," and leaned up against the corner of a building for the night. In the midst of his dozings a passer-by accosted him with, "Hello, Indian, aren't you lost?" to which he instantly replied: "No! Injun not lost, hotel lost!"

Abraham Enloe was a large stock-dealer for his day. It was his custom to drive annually horses, mules and cattle to southern markets, and by this and the acquisition of large tracts of land and the slave-trade, he accumulated considerable means and established a reputation at home, and in the marts of the south, for preeminent judgment and far-reaching business acumen.

He trafficked in negroes all the way from Western North Carolina to Florida. From the latter, on one occasion, he brought home twenty. He was kind to his slaves. A practical example of his benevolent policy toward them was shown in his habitual custom of reading and expounding to them the Holy Scriptures each Sabbath.

He is described by those who were intimate with him to have been possessed of a fund of anecdote. He was also rich in practical humor. When he would take the Sunday morning's "tansy-dram," of which the pioneer was famously though temperately fond, he would call up his little negroes, and causing them to stick out their big under lips, he would, with much dignity, pour a teaspoonful on each protruded lip to the infinite amusement of the family and the exquisite pleasure of the little ebonites themselves.

In his private life Abraham Enloe was cordially esteemed by his neighbors. In his family he ruled with patience and firmness. He was the father of nine sons and seven daughters. The sons all lived to man's estate, the only surviving one of whom says that each of the nine remained under parental control until he was of age, and not one was ever known to rebel against his father.

In personal appearance he is described by the family and those who knew him as having been a very large man, perhaps more, not less, than six feet high. Not corpulent but muscular and sinewy. His head was large and fine. Forehead, nose and mouth prominent. His hair was stiff and black. His complexion was inclined to tawny.

Unfortunately there is no likeness of him in existence. Men of his time didn't set much by pictures, and artists were scarce in the land.

He was undoubtedly a man of extraordinary mind. It is the universal consensus that he was the strongest character in his section, as a plain, practical, unaspiring citizen.

As heretofore intimated, his judgment was cheerfully deferred to or eagerly sought by his fellow citizens on subjects and occasions of moment.

He was simple, honest, brave; an ardent friend of truth. He hesitated not to go on toilsome errands of mercy for his bereft neighbors. He asked nothing in return but the answer of a good conscience. He was the best type of the civilian; plain, honest and unselfish. He had faults, but they were not such as rise from a mean heart plunged in moral turpitude, but those to which the flesh is easily heir. He was not a saint, but what is better here below, a nature's nobleman.

CHAPTER V.

ABRAHAM LINCOLN.

Born none knoweth when or where, he came up out of the bramble of obscurity. Whether he first saw the light in the woods, on the roadside, or in a dingy hovel, it matters not. He was nature's child, and nature nursed him. With her blessing she dropped him on the world and bade him live. He was first a helpless infant, then a little toddling child, and then a boy, but unlike other boys. He was awkward and gawky; his legs and arms were longer, his hands and feet were larger than those of other boys. He was more diffident and silent than any other boy.

At seven he went to school and learned to read; at ten he learned to write. He was serious and thoughtful; not overmuch energetic in body, but stint and duty urged him on, and he wielded the **ax** at the age of eight and did the milling.

Reaching youth he remained in school, procured books and applied himself diligently. He stepped at once to the head of his class, and when a pretty schoolmate, in spelling a word, hesitated to know whether to say *i* or *y*, he pointed to his eye, she spelled it, and the teacher, unobservant, passed on.

He loved books. He eagerly devoured all there were in the secular home library of three books and turned his eye in search of others. He made himself familiar with the best literature of the neighborhood for miles around. His nightly companions were such sacred, old standards as the Bible, Æsop's Fables, Robinson Crusoe, Bunyan's Pilgrim's Progress, and Weems's Life of Washington. He borrowed the latter from a penurious neighbor, placed it in the crack between the logs of the cabin overnight; there came a rain, which wet the book, and the boy carried it to the owner to assess the damage; the owner said seventy-five cents, and young Lincoln pulled fodder three days to satisfy him.

At the age of sixteen he wrote a dissertation on temperance and essayed poetry.

He grew to be a man, and he wanted, instead of his buckskin, a pair of brown jeans pantaloons, and he split for an old lady four hundred rails for every yard of cloth it took to make them. He read, he wrote, he spoke, he lectured, he farmed, he split rails, he pitched quoits, he joked, he wrestled, and sometimes he fought a fisticuff.

He became a surveyor; studied the statutes of Indiana and practiced stump-speaking in the fields to the hands.

He assisted in the management of a ferry across the Ohio river at thirty-seven and one-half cents a day; was noted as being the strongest man in the settlement, and was equally famous for writing papers on the science of government. He acted as bow-hand on a boat in a voyage to New Orleans at a salary of eight dollars a month, and made three thousand rails for one man, walking three miles each day to his work.

He was a religious free-thinker and an adept at anecdote. He became a loaf in New Salem, Illinois, and then clerk to an election board. He was a miller and then a clerk in a store.

He was a merchant, and studied English. He was a hero in an interesting love-affair, and came near fighting a duel.

He was captain of a company in the Black Hawk war and read law meanwhile.

He was elected to the Legislature, and later was admitted to the bar. He was one of the foremost lawyers in the State of Illinois, and the rival of Stephen A. Douglas for the heart of a charming blue-blooded girl; he vanquished the judge and obtained her hand in marriage.

He was a frequent contributor to political journals, and attained a local prominence as a campaigner and manager.

He was elected to Congress and never opened his mouth except to vote.

He stepped upon the hustings against the "Little Giant," and attracted the attention of the country by his resource and facility at repartee.

He was an orator of rare felicity, and a statesman of extraordinary sagacity.

He endeavored to lecture on "The History and Progress of Inventions" and ignominiously failed. He was invited to Cooper Institute to speak; he accepted the invitation, spoke on "The Political Issues of the Day," and paved his way to the presidency.

He was nominated for the Chief Magistracy of the nation over the trained diplomat and statesman, William H. Seward, and was elected over three other candidates, one of whom was his brilliant old-time rival, Stephen A. Douglas. He occupied the executive chair through the most horrible war of all history; was elected to a second term during the progress of that war, and just as he was adjusting his great faculties to lead the nation into a glorious peace, he was stricken by the red hand of an assassin.

History affords no parallel to Abraham Lincoln. In the classification of the world's heroes he must be grouped alone.

In the commingling and jargon of the common mass, he stood the tall representative of a new type.

His ways were of his own making. With his face set straight forward, his long arms swinging heavily, he strode so mightily that not only his own countrymen did list, but his footfall echoed around the world. Now he rose up, up, until he reached the heights, and then he grappled with the earth, and made those who touched him feel that they had touched a kindred clay.

His was a many-sided nature—an antithetical life—and his career was as mixed and varying as his nature was unique and odd.

Abraham Lincoln will never be understood.
He may be appreciated, but it will require an
exhaustive study of his character to enable
one to do so.

He possessed an intellect deep and keen.
He could see as far into profound and difficult
questions as any man contemporaneous with
him, or, doubtless, who has followed him.

He had a will—a will that was volatile or
immovable at the command of his soul. On
subjects of grave import his will, becoming
fixed, was not to be swerved a hair's breadth;
on questions indifferent and small his volition
was the obedient child of policy and expedi-
ency. His mind was no less subtle than logical in its operation. His judgment was as
clear and as unerring as mortal's usually is.

His heart was large, good and tender as a
child's. It was responsive in the highest and
best degree. No one in distress ever appealed
to him in vain. A great, picturesque rock in
a dry and thirsty land, the weary traveler
rested in its shade.

As Lincoln emerged from the wilderness
into civilization's highway men looked on
him and were amazed. Whence did he come
and whither was he bound? Lincoln beheld
their wonder. He read their very thought,
and herein was his mystery. In his intuitive
knowledge of men he towered, like the giant
he was, far above his fellows.

He early, how early we know not, became
conscious that he was *a man*, and learned to
associate with men as such. He did not have
to come down on the common human level—
he walked up and down between the clods
from which he sprang and to which he sadly
sank. In matters of conscience the angel of
the better nature was his guide. He was not
a Christian in the popular sense, traceable no-
doubt to his early bereavement of a mother.
He had no faith in the orthodox sense; his
faith was reason—the logic of cause and effect.
His reliance was firm in God and immortality;
his religion materialized in deeds whose end

was to make humanity better. He was not a
dreamer, but an intense practicalist. Of this
his life bore abundant evidence. By this it is
not meant that he could not scheme or plan
on the largest scale. This he did. But like
Alexander and Napoleon, he executed as rapidly as he planned. His genius was the most
fertile and versatile. No exigency arose to
confound his faculties and baffle his resource.
In the fiercest administrative storm he stood
on the topmost billow like a Norseman of old
unterrified. In the midst of these perplexi-
ties, when his associates were all dismay, he
related a humorous anecdote about some good
farmer in Illinois, and transformed the scene
of distraction into hilarious uproar.

He believed in the right and ability of mankind to govern themselves. He did not hesitate at the same time to avow "that all of the
people might do wrong part of the time."

He was a man of the most profound principle. He was preeminently a man of policy.
Principle was an end, policy was the means.

He was courageous physically, intellectually, morally. He shrank not from physical contests the most taxing.

He was eager to cross mental swords with the most brilliant.

He antagonized old, sacred beliefs in politics and religion with weird audacity, and his antagonist always bore away marks of the engagement.

He always weighed well his words and calculated coolly his acts; their effect was reckoned before they left him.   ·

He was ambitious. He was aspiring. He was restless. He sighted his object, and then thought and planned and strove to reach it.

He was certain of his powers, and he wielded them with a careful hand. There was no slumbering of talents with him; no rust nor ashes with the broken pottery of neglect in the paths he frequented.

Like some precious tree that regales the passer-by with its delightful perfume, he imparted a sweet influence to all who passed through the atmosphere of his being.

While others studied books, Lincoln studied men. Here was another and real secret of his life. From his plain Western home he looked abroad and surveyed the field. With a wise and cunning eye he looked at the East with her Phillips and her Sumner; the North with her Seward and her Cameron; the Middle and West with their Corwin and Chase; men of his own political party; men of vaulting ambition and commanding talent, and wondered how he might pass through them into the White House of the nation.

He outwitted, outthought, outdid a rival, no matter how great, and then looking back from the hill of success, he bound up that rival's broken hope by an unseen stratagem. Thus he made Secretaries, Generals, and Justices of the Supreme Court.

He was a superb tactician. He laid his plans with the utmost precision, and these rarely miscarried.

When he formulated a purpose he often con-
sulted the mind of others, but in the end he
preferred his own judgment, and upon it he
risked the issue.

He was frank and open in his general inter-
course, but there was a well-known line in his
character where publicity stopped and privacy
began. This discipline made his insight into
the public men with whom he dealt approxi-
mate omniscience. He knew their strong
points, their virtues, and he knew their faults
and foibles. He read their whims and their
caprices as one would read a book.

He unbosomed himself to none; he risked
many and trusted few. He collided with men
who, in some particular field, outshone him for
a moment, but it was only for a moment; he
had but to stand up and his simple personality
overshadowed them. There was but one
other person who possessed such simplicity
and majesty of character in our country, and
that was Robert E. Lee.

He knew the people—the plain folks, as he
was pleased to style them—as no man has
known them since the nation was born. He
was of them. Through the white portals of
the capitol of the republic he looked into the
lowly doors of millions of cabins each day of
his four years official incumbency. He saw
the struggle and toil; the grief and tears—he
felt them. As their faithful servant he remembered them and conducted their affairs
with a view to their peace, prosperity, and happiness. He knew their mode of thinking.
He was conversant with their manner of
speaking. He was familiar with their way of
acting. He thought, spoke and acted as if he
were in their presence. When he saluted
them or took them by the hand, there was a
meeting of friends. He was the prince of
plain men, and they were his neighbors. He
communicated with them in simplest speech
enlightened by homely illustration. With an
endless supply of fable and anecdote he amused
and instructed.

He loved and served the people, and the people loved and honored him. When it came to dealing with the people he had no patience with the time-server. He was bold when he dealt with the people. He invited the most rigid scrutiny of his public acts. He promulgated his conviction or policy, defended it through every stage of its progress, and if it failed of its object he acknowledged his mistake and assumed the responsibility. He sounded the public necessity and sought to satisfy it.

Trickery and simulation were foreign to him. If he thought he was being imposed upon, woe be to the impostor. If it was without his power to aid a friend, he frankly told him so.

He was charitable in the high catholic sense. He had a tender fellow-feeling for mankind. He knew the many weaknesses to which the flesh is heir. He was sure to see the suffering heart, and no one ever touched it more often to soothe.

He frequently withdrew from the multitude
and communed with himself. He came forth
stronger when he had encountered a difficulty.
He left the dross in the fire; sorrow and trib-
ulation were his earthly lot. "Myrrh and aloes
and ivory palaces" turned not his head; he
was touched but not influenced by praise; he
was often mortified but never unmanned by
criticism. The ludicrous filled him with life;
sorrow and suffering melted his heart.

He never fawned upon the public or an individual, and he was thought by some to be sel-
fish and austere. He never meddled with the
affairs of others, and he was accused of seeking
personal aggrandizement.

In the practice of the law he was natural
and urbane, and he was called a monkey and
a clown. He was cautious and conservative
in the exercise of his official functions, and he
was suspicioned and criticized by the impetuous who should have been his warmest friends.

As president, he was not impervious to adverse political criticism or personal detraction, and he made fewer mistakes than any man who has yet filled that exalted station.

In private life he was natural, original to the point of eccentricity.

He was by nature a melancholy man; he drew it from his mother. The purple lineaments of this inward ghost shone from his pale and haggard face. At times this spirit well-nigh overcame him, but he asserted his mighty will. He courted the nymph of humor; he gathered stories full of mirth and moral and told them to his company, and the wide prairie, the disordered law-office, or the executive chamber rang with jocund laughter.

He was a patient husband, a lenient, loving father. He was no conventionalist; he cared less than nothing for fad or fashion; he was insensible to gossip and had no part or lot in the little strivings of small men. With him there were no petty likes and dislikes—nothing mean or groveling. He hated a simper-

ing flatterer or growling churl with a mortal
hatred. He was forgiving, sympathetic, kind
—a broad-minded, great-hearted gentleman.

He was an American—the first American
illustrating the existence of a new national
type. He was the first popularly acknowledged representative of the plebeian cast; the
first prince of American peasants, and lifting
him upon their shoulders they proclaimed him
the first yeoman of their freehold.

Of Southern origin, born in the South, he
came up on a Western prairie. To Southern
inheritance was added Western environment.
To Southern warmth and generosity, springing
from Southern sun and soil, was added the
freedom of the Western plain and the rough
habits of Western life. He was by nature and
education the product of rural energy. The
South and West were the home of this element. Of this element Lincoln was the un-
trammeled child. His parents never dreamed
of Northern or Eastern sticklings for ancient

transatlantic customs and laws. Such were his early surroundings, and so soon did he leave the South that he never had any prepossessions in favor of human slavery.

He was the simple though strong individual, and then the oracle of his class—the masses everywhere. The blessings of his virtuous mind and provident hand in due time began to fall upon all. His influence no partizanship could destroy or faction avoid.

He was a patriot. He loved his country for his country's sake. He sought to cement the common interest and advance the common weal.

He was a steadfast believer in, and supporter of, the Constitution. He studied and construed it. He advocated a perpetual Union, and would not admit the right of any State to withdraw from it. He labored · as no man ever has or will to preserve the Union unimpaired. This was the sole and only object of his chief magisterial life. He was opposed to

the extension of human slavery into new territory, but "it was never his inclination or
purpose to interfere with that institution in
the States where it did exist." He deprecated
the idea of freeing the colored race and turn-
ing them loose, clothed with equal rights,
among the white people of the South. If he
had lived it never would have been done. He
was the great central, controlling spirit on the
Union side, and he waged the war on purely
defensive grounds. The noble people of the
North and East, though blood of our blood,
did not realize the situation. Their splendid
humanitarianism was too long-ranged. Not
by striking the shackles from the colored race,
for that was right, but by making him the
equal of all of us whom they would not acknowledge the equal of a single man of them,
they decreed that we should wander in the
wilderness of problem and uncertainty, not
forty years, but indefinitely. Lincoln understood this, and his great heart went out in

sympathy for the bleeding South. He knew that he was the son of her bosom and that her children were his brethren.

He labored as long as there was a shadow of hope to avert war. When its crimson tide began to flow, he proposed to buy the slaves and stop it. Failing in this, he endeavored to colonize them beyond the choler of unhappy memory and the antipathy of strange blood.

Persistent, firm and gentle in his memory of the South, he bore up against the pressure from the North to arm the black man against his former master. But when at last he saw that unless something was done, his fondest dream would come to naught, he reluctantly gave way, and a portion of the slaves were made to lift their hands against us.

The stricken South lost this noble friend— her filial scion—when least she could afford it. Wilkes Booth might well have stayed the deadly hand, for if he had the South had journeyed round the valley through which she is passing. But happily the time is now when the generous people of the North and East who, with the wisdom of prophecy, picked Mr. Lincoln up at his opportunity and placed him where God intended, are seeing their mistake, and with the same candor and zeal which marked their strife to bring about our problem, are essaying to help us solve it.

America has produced and will produce but one Lincoln. The world may now see but shall not soon understand this enigmatical man.

CHAPTER VI.

THE ENLOES.

It is not only interesting but of historical importance to produce, in this connection, a short account of the Enloe family.

This family does not lay claim to a niche in the nation's Westminster, nor does it accept a plat in its potter's field. It rather takes its place in the cemetery of honor and respectability. This is not meant to refer so much to descent as to position in society. It is not our object to lay for it "claim to long descent." This doubtless would bring with it some difficulty, and yet it would be no more difficult in the case of the Enloes than in that of any other ordinary family of the English-speaking people.

In support of this last proposition, permit me to quote a no less eminent authority than

MRS. ANDREW J. PATTON.

Daughter of Wesley Enloe.

Justice Walter Clark: "William the Conqueror ascended the throne of England A. D.
1066. Allowing thirty-three years as a generation, there have been twenty generations,
counting his children then living as the first
generation. Many people have several children, others have more. It is certainly not
an immoderate calculation to average each
descendant as having three children, for if each
descendant with his wife had left only two
children, the population would have stood still,
whereas less than a million inhabitants of the
British Isles of that day have grown to be
nearly forty millions there and seventy millions on this side of the water. William the
Conqueror had four sons and six daughters;
averaging each of these as having three children, with the same average for each of their
descendants down to the present, and the ten
children of William in the present or twenty-
fifth generation, by a simple arithmetical calculation, would have 2,824,295,314,810 de-

scendants now living in the British Isles, in America, in the colonies, or wherever men of British descent are to be found.

As this is fully twenty-five thousand times as many as there are people of British descent on the globe, there must be an error in the above calculation. There are two. First: While an average of two children to each descendant is too small, since that average would have kept the population stationary, an average of three is too high, as that is an increase of fifty per cent. every thirty years, an average which few countries other than the United States could show.

The second error is that intermarriages among descendants must be allowed for. Say that owing to these errors the result of the calculation is twenty thousand times too much, it would still result that every man of English-speaking race is descended from the Conqueror. Reduce it as much more as you like and the chances are yet strong that any given man of

MRS. FLOYD.

Granddaughter of Abraham Enloe.

your acquaintance, as well as yourself, is probably a descendant of the victor of Hastings."

Apropos to this the distinguished Judge says, and truly: "The doctrine of heredity has some force in it, but much that is called heredity is simply the effect of environment."

There is much of interest here in the study of the character of Abraham Lincoln, especially as viewed from the North Carolina tradition. The history of the Enloes, from its remotest period, illustrates the force of a wise selection, both as to heredity and environment. This is shown most clearly in the ease with which they have held their own in the race for Anglo-Saxon supremacy. From the time of their coming to the Colonies from across the water until now, their history shows that they have occupied the same stable, reputable station in society—the best circle of the middle class; the class that constitutes the salt of civilization, the saving-grace element of the race.

Three Enloe brothers, forebears of the family, landed about the middle of the seventeenth century, in Maryland. They came from Scotland and England. One of these brothers settled on Lord Baltimore's land, and reared a family. The other two went from Maryland to South Carolina and made their home in York district.

These old Enloes were school-teachers by profession—men of liberal education. From these three men have sprung a numerous progeny, scattered over Maryland, South Carolina, North Carolina, Georgia, Tennessee, Kentucky, Illinois, Missouri, California and Texas. It is remarkable the number of strong men throughout this long line. We fearlessly invite any one who may feel skeptical as to this assertion to investigate for himself.

All down the line from the day when the South Carolina grandsires began to "train the young idea to shoot," to the present when they sit in State legislatures, in Congress and upon the bench, the Enloes have undoubtedly contributed materially to the building of the Republic. They have marched in the forefront of frontier settlement, undaunted by the sternest difficulties. They have introduced civil government in the wilderness, and modestly, yet liberally, contributed to the support of its institutions. They have helped make, construe and enforce the laws by which they have been governed. Wherever duty called, in peace or war, they have cheerfully responded.

Wherever they have dwelt, they have distinguished themselves for intelligence, industry and probity. Wherever they have planted themselves, thrifty farmers, successful merchants, physicians, jurists and legislators have sprung up.

Physically they are rather large, tall, slender, but raw-boned as a rule, and sinewy. Mentally they are vigorous and alert, and throughout the line, in an individual here and there, there is a vein of natural humor. One instance

I recall now : Matthew Enloe, deceased, son of Abraham Enloe, was not an educated man, owing to poor early advantages, but being possessed of a fine, native intellect he enlivened the company with which he was thrown with a sparkling humor. We have been assured by those who knew him well that he was even more like Abraham Lincoln in personal appearance than is his surviving brother Wesley. We confess, however, that this is hard to conceive after seeing only the latter.

We shall here offer the interesting letters of three representatives of the Enloe family, residing respectively in North Carolina, Illinois and Missouri. These letters are the more interesting because the North Carolina representative, as we are led to infer from the circumstances, when he wrote knew nothing of the Illinois or Missouri Enloes, and when the Illinois and Missouri representatives wrote neither of them knew anything of the North Carolina Enloes. And what is still more interest-

CAPT. WILLIAM A. ENLOE.
Grandson of Abraham Enloe.

ing, in this place, is the proof which these letters afford of the general accuracy of tradition, together with the commendable pride and care with which the Enloes preserve their name and family identity :

DILLSBORO, N. C., January 28, 1899.
Jas. H. Cathey, Esq., Sylva, N. C.

MY DEAR SIR :—Your letter found me in the grasp of the grippe, but I shall be pleased to answer your questionos as best I can.

My ancestors were of Scotch and English descent as far as I have been able to trace them. They came to this country (that is, direct) from England.

My father's given name was Scroup. This name was always a mystery to me on account of its peculiarity. I could not account for it until I came across it in an old English history. I found in this history that there once lived in England a family whose surname was Scroup, and that they owned a large estate which descended under that name.

On finding this name in English history, and recalling that neither I nor any one else whom I had ever met in this country had ever heard of the name Scroup outside of my immediate family, I became quite convinced, the originals having set sail from there, that my family on some side were of English stock.

From the best information I have, there were three brothers of the original Enloes who came from the old country. They made their first stop in Maryland, where one of them staid and raised a family. One of them emigrated to York District, South Carolina. This was my great-grandfather. I think his name was Gilbert.

My grandfather, Abraham Enloe, came over to Rutherford county, North Carolina, and married there a Miss Egerton. He afterward moved just above the Indian Mission, then to Ocona Lufta, in Buncombe county, where he resided till his death. He raised nine sons and seven daughters. The other

CAPT. WM. A. ENLOE

At at Earlier Age.

brother of my great-grandfather, and one of
the original three, went to Middle Tennessee
and settled. He raised a considerable family.
One of his descendants, B. A. Enloe, represented the Eighth Tennessee district in Congress for several successive terms.

Some of the Yorkville branch of the family
moved to Georgia and elsewhere. Those in
Georgia got to spelling their name "Inlow,"
instead of Enloe. I visited the old gentleman—the head of the Georgia branch. I
found we were of the same stock. He told
me that when he went to Georgia, people
there were inclined to spell the name "Inlow"; they kept it up; he did not file his ob-
jection, and he finally found himself illustrating the doctrine that custom eventually
becomes law, and writing it himself the same
way.

Judge Enloe, who was assassinated at Elli-
jay, Georgia, by "bushwhackers," during the
war, was this old gentleman's son. Hon. W.

Burder Ferguson, of Waynesville, N. C., read law under Judge Enloe.

As to my grandfather Abraham Enloe's intelligence, he was naturally of strong mind, and was well educated for a man of his time. He was a justice of the peace, an office of no little importance in pioneer days. He did the official writing for his neighborhood.

Yours truly,

WILLIAM A. ENLOE.

MULBERRY GROVE, ILL., Sept. 16, 1895.
Jas. H. Cathey, Esq., Sylva, N. C.

DEAR SIR:—Yours of the 14th inst. to hand, and I hasten to reply.

I am unable to throw any light on the subject of Lincoln's origin, further than looks—physical appearance.

Abe Lincoln was a long, bony man, as are all the Enloes I have ever seen. As to his father being an Enloe, I know nothing.

I will now give you, as near as I can, a brief history of my part of the Enloe family.

My father's name was James; his father's
name was Ashael; his father was Isaac Enloe, a Scotchman. Isaac Enloe was a Revolutionary patriot and soldier. There were
two brothers of the old Scotch stock who settled in York county, South Carolina. My
father and grandfather moved to Davidson
county, Tenn., I think about the year 1808,
where my grandfather Ashael taught school.
(See history of Davidson county, Tenn.)
About the year 1816 they moved to Illinois,
where we have remained ever since.

As to myself, I served through the entire
war, '61–5, in an Illinois regiment. I was
not in North Carolina during the war, but
had a brother who was with Sherman there.
I was a First Lieutenant in the Gulf Depart-
ment after Vicksburg, and I will say that although I fought the South for nearly four
years, and got mixed up with the Johnnies in
many an unpleasant place (at least to me), I
was never captured until years after Lee quit

at Appomattox. In 1871 I was taken in by
a North Carolina gal. She waged a war on
the aggressive, and came all the way to Illinois to get to capture me. Her father was in
the Confederate army. I think this is as it
should be—mix the people up and put an end
to difference and distance.

I will send you a letter I received some
time ago from Dr. Isaac N. Enloe, of Jefferson
City, Missouri. Hope this may be of some
service to you.

Respectfully yours,

SAM G. ENLOE.

JEFFERSON CITY, MO., May 5, 1894.
Sam G. Enloe, Mulberry Grove, Ill.

DEAR SIR:—Your letter in regard to our
family and relationship to hand. I am satisfied we are of the same stock.

From my oldest brother, James, who has
heard my grandfather speak of his ancestors,
I have the following: The first of the Enloe

J. FRANK ENLOE.

Son of Wesley and Grandson of Abe Enloe.

stock or family, consisting of two brothers
named Isaac and Enoch, both school-teachers,
settled in South Carolina. Previous to going
to South Carolina they lived for a while,
teaching, in Maryland. This was some time
near the middle of the seventeenth century.
Both originally came from Scotland. My
great-grandfather Enoch was the son of one
of these Enloe brothers; Isaac, I think. I
have no positive information to that effect, but
my great-grandfather must have had brothers.
Isaac and Enoch Enloe both married in
South Carolina and raised large families.
One of these families became quite wealthy
and remained in that State. Members of the
other family, about the year 1808, moved to
Tennessee. In 1808 my grandfather moved
from South Carolina to Tennessee. My
grandfather married a sister of his brother
Isaac's wife. Isaac had three sons, Benjamin,
James and Joel. Ben still lives in Tennessee,
and is the father of Benjamin A. Enloe, Con-

gressman from the eighth Tennessee district. James and Joel are physicians, and reside in Nashville, Tenn.

My grandfather, James Enloe, was born in York district, South Carolina, February 19th, 1793. He moved from there to Tennessee in 1808, and in 1828 he moved to Missouri. In Missouri he entered land and farmed, devoting no little time to horses and politics. He represented Cole county in the State Legislature once, and Moniteau, after it was cut off from Cole, twice.

My father Enoch was born in Barren county, Kentucky, in 1814, where my grandfather had moved temporarily. He came with grandfather to Missouri in 1828. My father married a Miss Murray. Of this union there were, in all, fourteen children. Eleven lived to be grown—seven sons and four daughters. One of my brothers is a merchant, two of us are physicians, and the others are farmers.

Yours truly, ISAAC N. ENLOE.

In this letter of Dr. I. N. Enloe ·we have eliminated a great deal relating to his immediate family, of the Enloes. ʃWe have meant simply to trace the name toward its original. There are, however, two things we have left out which we deem worthy of mention here— the frequent appearance of Abraham, showing that it was a common name in the Enloe family, and the certain indication that the Enloes were superstitiously observant of the scriptural injunction, " to be fruitful and multiply, and replenish the earth, and subdue it."

It is only just to say that each of the foregoing letters is a courteous response to urgent and repeated solicitations.

CHAPTER VII.

WISDOM AND PROPHECY.

From Mr. Lincoln's Inaugural Address of 4th March, 1861 :—

My countrymen, one and all, think calmly and well upon this whole subject. Nothing valuable can be lost by taking time. If there be an object to hurry any of you in hot haste to a step which you would never take deliberately, that object will be frustrated by taking time; but no good object can be frustrated by it. Such of you as are now dissatisfied still have the old Constitution unimpaired, and on the sensitive point, the laws of your own framing under it, while the new administration will have no immediate power, if it would, to change either. If it were admitted that you who are dissatisfied hold the right side in the dispute, there still is no single good reason for precipitate action. Intelligence, patriotism, Christianity and a firm reliance on Him who has never yet forsaken his favored land, are still competent to adjust in the best way all our present difficulty.

In your hands, my dissatisfied fellow-countrymen, and not in mine, is the momentous issue of civil war. The government will not assail you. You can have no conflict without being yourselves the aggressors. You have no oath registered in Heaven to destroy the government, while I shall have the most solemn oath to "preserve, protect and defend it."

I am loath to close. We are not enemies, but friends. We must not be enemies. Though passion may have strained, it cannot break our bonds of affection. The mystic cord of memory, stretching from every battle-field and patriot grave to every living heart and hearth-stone all over this broad land, will yet swell the chorus of the Union, when again touched,

as surely they will be, by the better angels of
our nature.

———————

From his famous letter to Horace Greeley :—

As to the policy I "seem to be pursuing,"
as you say, I have not meant to leave any one
in doubt. I would save the Union. I would
save it in the shortest way under the Constitution. The sooner the national authority can
be restored the nearer the Union will be—the
Union as it was.

If there be those who would not save the
Union unless they could at the same time
destroy slavery, I do not agree with them.

My paramount object is to save the Union,
and not either to save or to destroy slavery.

If I could save the Union without freeing
any slave, I would do it—if I could save it by
freeing all the slaves, I would do it—if I could
save it by freeing some and leaving others alone,
I would do that. What I do about slavery and
the colored race, I do because it helps to save
the Union.

From his message of March 6, 1862:—

I recommend the adoption of a resolution by your honorable body, which shall be substantially as follows:

Resolved, That the United States, in order to co-operate with any State which may adopt gradual abolition of slavery, give to such State pecuniary aid, to be used by such State, in its discretion, to compensate it for the inconvenience, public and private, produced by such change of system.

———

On the 14th August, 1862, he received a deputation of colored men, with whom he held an interview on the subject of colonization, in which he, among other things, said:—

It now becomes my duty, as it has long been my inclination, to favor the colonization of the people of African descent residing in the United States. Why should the people of your race be colonized, and where? Why should they leave this country? This, perhaps, is the first question for proper consideration. You and we are different races. We have between us a broader difference than exists between almost any other two races. Whether it is right or wrong I need not discuss; but this physical difference is a great disadvantage to us both, as I think.

Your race suffer very greatly, many of them by living among us, while ours suffer from your presence. In a word, we suffer on each side.

If this is admitted, it affords a reason, at least, why we should be separated.

You, here, are freemen, I suppose. Perhaps you have long been free, or all your lives. Your race are suffering, in my judgment, the greatest wrong inflicted on any people. But even when you cease to be slaves, you are yet far removed from being placed on an equality with the white race. You are cut off from many of the advantages which the white race enjoys. The aspiration of men is to enjoy equality with the best when free, but on this broad continent not a

single man of your race is made the equal of
a single man of ours. Go where you are
treated the best, and the ban is still upon you.
I do not propose to discuss this, but I treat it as
a fact with which we have to deal. I cannot
alter it if I would. . It is the fact about which
we all think and feel alike, I and you.

We look to our condition. Owing to the existence of two races on this continent, I need
not recount to you the effects upon white men
growing out of the institution of slavery. I
believe in its general evil effects on the white
race. See our present condition—the country
engaged in a war! our white men cutting one-
another's throats; none knowing how far it
will extend, and then consider what we know
to be the truth. But for your race among us
there could not be war, although many men
engaged on either side do not care for you one
way or the other.

Nevertheless, I repeat, without the institution of slavery, and the colored race as a basis,

the war could not have an existence. It is
better for us both, therefore, that we be separated.

His speech on the occasion of the dedication of the
battle-field of Gettysburg :—

Four score and seven years ago our fathers brought forth on this continent a new nation, conceived in liberty and dedicated to the
proposition that all men are created equal.
Now we are engaged in a great civil war, test-
ing whether that nation so dedicated can long
endure. We are met on a great battle-field of
that war. We have come to dedicate a portion of that field as a final resting-place for
those who here gave their lives that that nation
might live. It is altogether fitting and proper
that we should do this.

But in a larger sense we cannot dedicate—
we cannot consecrate—we cannot hallow this
ground. The brave men who struggled here
have consecrated it far above our poor power
to add or detract. The world will little note

nor long remember what we *say* here, but it can never forget what they *did* here. It is for us, the living, rather to be dedicated here to the unfinished work which they who fought here have thus far so nobly advanced. It is, rather for us to be here dedicated to the great task remaining before us, that from these honored dead we take increased devotion for which they gave the last full measure of devotion; that we here highly resolve that these dead shall not have died in vain ; that this nation under God shall have a new birth of freedom; and that government of the people, by the people, for the people, shall not perish from the earth.

———

NOTE:—For the foregoing extracts, except the Gettysburg address, the author is under obligation to Raymond's Life of Lincoln.

CHAPTER VIII.

ADDENDA.

PART I.   AUTHOR'S INTRODUCTION.

Since the making of this little book interest has steadily increased in the subject of the paternal origin of Abraham Lincoln, and the public faith has as steadily waxed in the theory upheld by this narrative. The book has passed through two editions; the last is now exhausted and the third, containing additional, vital evidence, is this you hold in your hand.

Every statement of fact in this volume is the solemn statement of persons—intelligent admirers of Mr. Lincoln—the equal of the most conservative, trustworthy and patriotic in the country.

The first two editions have circulated in every State in the Union; have gone to Canada, Mexico, England, Scotland and India.

The author has received letters by the hundred from representative citizens manifesting much interest in the facts thus made public for the first time. Not a few of these letters are from gentlemen familiar with the time and men contemporaneous with Mr. Lincoln, some of whom knew Mr. Lincoln personally. Distinguished scholars, divines, statesmen and publicists of all sections have evinced previous knowledge of the existence of a foundation for this record, and attach unmistakable credence thereto.

Truth is, historic record and the public voice this narrative has elicited, unite in showing that the public have been incredulous of the chapter on the paternal origin of Abraham Lincoln as written by his popular biographers.

No biography is complete, no biography is faithful that has not an open, ringing announcement of the parentage of the subject.

Mr. Lincoln's biographers may be divided into two groups touching his parentage: The first, those about whom the light had shone and whose sense of honor and professional responsibility forbade their passing unnoted the fact that light revealed; and the second, those who knew nor cared, more than to apotheosize their subject.

Less than four of Mr. Lincoln's hundreds of biographers make up the first class. Neither class has produced an authentic biography. The first are the victim of a reckless credulity and unnatural public sentiment; the second have not the full courage of their conviction.

Messrs. John Locke Scripps, William H. Herndon and Ward H. Lamon are the first class.

Mr. Scripps was Mr. Lincoln's first biographer and obtained his information from Mr. Lincoln's own lips.

Mr. Herndon was Mr. Lincoln's law-partner and intimate personal friend of more than a quarter of a century. Mr. Lamon, in addition to the benefit of Mr. Lincoln's personal acquaintance, had unrestricted use of the original manuscript of Mr. Herndon. These three enjoyed peculiar advantages for writing an authentic personal biography of Abraham Lincoln.

Mr. Scripps wrote at a time when his estimate must, necessarily, have been shallow and incomplete. Mr. Herndon enjoyed a much wider and calmer perspective. Mr. Lamon came into possession of fruits of the labors of both, added to his own research, verification and contemplation. But neither of these has shown himself an ideal biographer of Abraham Lincoln. They have evinced fatal lack of industry, courage and candor. Abraham Lincoln was, in the last analysis, the soul of these virtues. If the life of any man in human annals is entitled to fidelic record it is that of Abraham Lincoln. His distinguishing mark was the fidelity his character bore to the mother that brought him forth—his life-likeness to the old Earth.

In simple naturalness, unadulterated plainness he stands alone, not quite approached by any other great man of history. Even his physical form was so plain that it verged upon the grotesque. The movement of his body and action of his mind were ordered by the laws of simplicity, freedom and truth. No human dogma, however universal, could have influenced him against his conviction any more than it could have influenced the currents of the wind or the sea. His soul was the remorseless hater of sham and counterfeit and error, and that which maketh a lie in any and every guise.

There is not another such composition in ancient or modern annals. There is no other so profound a study. Withal, to the patient and faithful and courageous he is possible of solution. Once the correct vantage-ground is reached there is serene and satisfying contemplation. Nowhere is there promise of larger reward for diligent investigation. The unknowable in him is a small and unimportant moiety.

Hitherto the world has been unable to account for Abraham Lincoln's being, reasoning from orthodox, human hypotheses. His origin and antecedents may be known. His advent into the world was not miraculous. He never claimed supernatural origin. He came into the world, primarily, as all other human beings come. If he were the child of a special providence, so be it. He was the child of natural parents. True he was the hero of a crisis. Like the Conqueror, and Cromwell, and Luther, and Wesley, the creator of an era—the cohesive spirit of a world-movement. But, after all, he was no more divine or inspired than they. He was intensely human with a superlatively fine moral fiber—fine as that of Washington; rudimentarily as fine as that of Robert Edward Lee—two of the climaxes of human perfection in sixty centuries.

Events of his remarkable career bear witness to his sustained fidelity to the loftier human instincts — instincts inherent and schooled in the university of nature—nature in her best estates. Nature was always jealous of Abraham Lincoln. He acknowledged no master and but one mistress—Nature. In boyhood he played the innocent pranks and dreamt the roseate dreams of that happy estate; in manhood to the tragic end he played with nature's master hand upon the harp of the souls of men. An upright appreciation of these primal elements of Abraham Lincoln's character, as well as a due regard for the rights of posterity should prompt his biographer to adopt as his criterion the well known rule of Cicero : "Neither dare to say anything that is false or fear to say anything that is true, nor give any just suspicion of favor or disaffection."

A fit biographer of Abraham Lincoln shall be the man of rugged honesty and patient intrepidity—a Boswell in detail, a Carlyle in faith, even if " Boswell must be paid for showing his bear," and if Carlyle must moil for "seventeen years in the valley of the shadow of Frederick."

Time may not yet be full for a just biographical portraiture of Abraham Lincoln. But there is no danger in asserting that hitherto his biographers have been provincial in concept and partizan in expression.

The work of Mr. Wm. H. Herndon approaches most nearly the exception.

The first (in point of time) biographies of Mr. Lincoln are necessarily shallow and inaccurate. These were written in haste from motives of personal and party interest.

The saner judgment of his biographer of more recent years has been eclipsed by the nearness of the marvelous events of his official career, the magnitude of the results of the crisis in which Providence ordained him the principal factor, and his own strange, gigantic, fascinating personality.

In short, four things have combined to prevent the real life of Abraham Lincoln : blind hero-worship; aristocratic sentiment; false modesty and aversion to laborious research—four things Abraham Lincoln trampled under his feet as an elephant would trample the mire of the jungle.

Little wonder Abraham Lincoln's origin has been the subject of imagination and conjecture. In childhood and youth his place of abode a squalid camp in a howling wilderness; his meal an ashen crust; his bed a pile of leaves; his nominal guardian a shiftless and worthless wanderer; his intimate associates and putative relatives a gross, illiterate and superstitious rabble.

Little wonder that in some quarters Abraham Lincoln's fame has bordered upon deification. His all but miraculous burst from the wilderness into the nation's eye; his heroic and glorious life-achievement; his sudden passing at the assassin's hand, these, with the element of sadness which was the inseparable genius of his nature and culminating incident of his fortune, are the elements needful to magnify the subject beyond human proportion. Abraham Lincoln passed from the mountain top of earthly greatness into the vast unknown in a halo of heroism, mysticism and sorrow; and doubtless he shall continue for all time to come to draw from all mankind admiration, wonder and tears. In the glamor of this mingled mist and glare the huge proportion of one of the greatest and most human of men has been despoiled by the rude hand of the ignorant enthusiast. The great, refreshing spectacle has been bungled. The pity of it! As a result of the operation of these abnormal influences the entire life of Abraham Lincoln has suffered, but no chapter like that on his origin. Here was something out of the ordinary—something unseen; but instead of allowing the light to shine into this grotto in a great life, fanatic biographers and other sinister and designing persons, have endeavored to magnify and involve the mystery for purposes of heathen worship, or have sought to come into possession of it that they might destroy it. The paternal origin of Abraham Lincoln: this is the secret. Light, once deflected here and an hundred other nooks and corners in his personality, will light up and become plain and comprehensible.

To evade or conceal a cardinal fact relative to Abraham Lincoln is not only a moral wrong, but a reflection upon his character and a violation of his memory. The nature of his origin is primarily indispensable to an intelligent, not to say full, conception of his character. The correct source of his origin is, practically, universally accepted as a matter of doubt—an unsettled question—an unknown quantity—in his life. If no trustworthy means were in existence or accessible for the removal of the doubt, for the settlement of the question, moral responsibility would not obtain and the mystery would continue. But, fortunately for posterity, there is in existence and available all the means necessary to a final, correct and satisfactory solution. Using the approved methods of the historian in collecting data, there is not a fact in the first twenty years of the life of Abraham Lincoln easier of establishment than that of his real paternal origin.

There could be but three ways of accounting for the being of Abraham Lincoln or any other man: First, that he was of natural legitimate origin; second, that he was of natural illegitimate origin; and third, that he was of miraculous origin. The first hypothesis has been taken for granted as true and passed without further thought by the casual layman and biographical novice. The second hypothesis or theory has been affirmed by tradition so well defined, closely connected and emphatic that the element of myth is entirely absent; by the two most intimate and distinguished personal biographers of Mr. Lincoln after the most laborious, exhaustive and conscientious research; and by an extensive, intelligent and authentic public consensus. .The third hypothesis has been *whispered* by the few, and *voiced* by at least one reputable eulogist who said that "*Abraham Lincoln was without ancestors, fellows or successors.*" It is barely possible that some of Mr. Watterson's contemporaries should construe him literally, and that mankind generally a thousand years hence would do so, it is more than probable. Granted that the third hypothesis is unreasonable, the settlement of the question turns upon the weight of evidence between the first and second.

It is the office of these pages to submit testimony in support of the second theory—that Abraham Lincoln was of illegitimate origin, his father being Abraham Enloe, and not Thomas Lincoln or any one else.

In addition to the sound, sustained and perennial tradition of North Carolina, the author submits in this addenda extrinsic historical data and other cumulative evidence.

————————

Before giving to the public the record of the paternity of Abraham Lincoln in the present enlarged form, we desire to say that the data bearing upon the subject is cumulative, and promises to continue to be for an indefinite time. There is other material now in sight, but inaccessible for the present, or at all, without the expenditure of much time and no little money.

This enlarged edition is the result of the acquisition of several years, and, when time and opportunity permits, facts that may come to light that are worth while, will be included in a subsequent edition. Now that this investigation has been begun it is our duty to accept, preserve and publish all the material, trustworthy facts bearing upon the subject.

Two things, we contend, our research have disclosed beyond question : First, that Abraham Lincoln was illegitimate, and second, that his father was an Abraham Enloe.

Another thing is clear as a result of our research : That there has been a determined and systematic effort on the part of at least two of Mr. Lincoln's most intimate personal biographers to discover the truth of his paternal origin and publish the same to the world —these biographers were William H. Herndon, his law partner, and Ward H. Lamon.

Again, there is another fact that is, as a

result of this investigation, equally as certain : That there has been a determined and systematic war of suppression and destruction against the publication and dissemination of the truth of Mr. Lincoln's real paternal origin by certain individuals.

It was the original purpose of Mr. Wm. H. Herndon to write a rigidly truthful narrative of the life of Abraham Lincoln. How much this purpose was influenced or prevented is a matter that is familiar to persons now living.

Mr. Jessie W. Weik, of Greencastle, Indiana, toward the last in the preparation of his biography, became a collaborator with Mr. Herndon. In 1865 Mr. Herndon visited the scenes of Mr. Lincoln's birth and early years in Kentucky, as did Mr. Weik, later.

These personal visits to Kentucky were made with a view to ascertaining the *truth* pertaining to these early periods in the life of their hero. Mr. Herndon says that "Mr. Weik spent considerable time investigating the truth of a report current in Bourbon county, Kentucky, that Thomas Lincoln from one Abraham Inlow, a miller there, assumed the paternity of the infant child of a poor girl named Nancy Hanks, and after marriage, moved with her to Washington or Hardin county, where the son, who was named Abraham, after his real, and Lincoln after his putative father, was born." Mr. Herndon does not say that Mr. Weik after investigation, found the report to be untrue, but, instead, goes on at considerable length to substantiate the report.

See *suppressed* matter following.

This much may be found in the suppressed three-volume edition of Lincoln by Messrs. Herndon and Weik. The question then recurs upon the fact as to whether there was an elaborate investigation of the illegitimate paternity of Mr. Lincoln, and if so, did they write down in their manuscript for posterity, the complete account of their findings. The facts are that Mr. Weik, because of influences brought to bear upon him, receded from his original position of independent recorder of truth and fact and destroyed the original manuscript.

Mr. Lamon bought from Mr. Herndon the

use of his original manuscript, paying him three thousand dollars therefor.

But Mr. Weik and those associated with him in their campaign of destruction, were careful to make way with every volume of Lamon they could lay hand on.

Through Weik's influence other valuable evidence gathered by Mr. Herndon at great expense was destroyed.

It will be noted that the facts touching Abraham Lincoln's illegitimate origin as first recorded by his intimate friend and law partner between whom and Mr. Lincoln, as Mr. Horace White assures us, there was never an unkind word or thought, are three editions removed from Mr. Herndon's original manuscript. The Lamon biography which we count as one edition, it having within its covers the original Herndon manuscript, the three-volume Life by Messrs. Herndon and Weik, and the two-volume edition by Messrs. Herndon and Weik.

It is evident that the three-volume edition was suppressed because of the statements with regard to Mr. Lincoln's illegitimate paternity, for the reason that these are the identical statements expurgated in the last or two-volume edition of Herndon and Weik.

It is establishable that the collaborator of Mr. Herndon, who was the collector of this illegitimate-paternity data, was also the chief agent in the destruction of it. It is even more remarkable that the current expurgated edition in two volumes contains numerous hints of illegitimate paternity but in very subdued form.

These facts evidently show that the original findings of William H. Herndon and Jesse W. Weik, upon the question of Abraham Lincoln's paternity, were indubitable. This being admitted the facts which were published in meager or subdued form would indicate the facts which were written or published in complete or elaborate form.

And more, is it reasonable that two reputable citizens, cultured and refined gentlemen, the one the law-partner and life-long, intimate friend, and the other an ardent admirer, of a man among the greatest and most illustrious of the time, would, as his personal biographers, write down for the gaze of posterity a *rumor*, a *report* affecting so personal and vital a subject as that of his origin, and that, too, in defiance of the well-known canons of society?

In view of these facts the conclusion is inevitable, leaving the North Carolina tradition entirely out of the question, that Abraham Lincoln was the son of an Abraham Enloe by Nancy Hanks.

We shall not discuss the question of Mr. Lincoln's illegitimate paternity from the Lamon biography point of view further than to invite the reader's careful attention to the entire quotation on the subject, and particularly to the allusions to the relations existing between Thomas Lincoln and *Abraham* Enloe or Inlow, the name being spelled differently in different localities.

Mr. Lamon's opening paragraphs are significant. He says almost emphatically that Lincoln was of illegitimate paternity. He wrote in the major part from Mr. Herndon's manuscript, and it is evident that he *knew* that Abraham Lincoln was an illegitimate.

Subsequent references to the "Inlows," and to "Abraham Inlow," afford strong reason for the inference that he knew to a certainty the fact he had obliquely though unmistakably stated at the outset.

It were far better had Messrs. Herndon and Weik and Mr. Lamon written and published the plain, blunt facts. By recording a rumor, a vague report, these biographers lowered, vulgarized and jeopardized their office. If, as it is our opinion based upon thorough investigation, these biographers wrote down the true facts about Mr. Lincoln's origin, and these facts were afterward modified and accommodated by others to the end that they might be shadowed with doubt, and ultimately ignored by the student of Abraham Lincoln, the perpetrators misjudged mankind and threw a challenge in the teeth of the very incident they were designing to intercept. Somewhere in the deep of the heart of mankind there is a chamber sacred to the love of truth. The tallest and whitest heroes of history are the martyrs to the cause of truth.

The most universally popular of the works of literature is the book of truth.

Had the Bible depicted only the fair, the favored and the far-famed side of its characters—its priests and prophets, its heroes and poets, its rulers and its peoples—it had long ago been torn into ten thousand times its number of apparent inconsistencies, and scattered to the four winds of heaven. Then indeed would a Voltaire or an Ingersoll have had a pic-nic. But it deals with every one of its characters, save Christ the Lord, as a human, and records the truth and the *whole* truth about each. This is the secret, from the human side, of the solidity and force of the book, this is one quality which led Mr. Gladstone to characterize it as "The impregnable rock of the Holy Scriptures." If it were anything short of one connected tissue of truth, pleasant and unpleasant, it had not merited the striking metaphor.

So long as men are treated as human there is no reason for the distortion, misrepresentation or suppression of the facts relating to their lives. In an enlightened country, such as ours, to deify any man, however great, will prove quite a difficult if not a hazardous undertaking. Our age is an age of faith based upon sight, truth and practicality. Candor and honesty are more attractive than mist and falsehood.

It is an age when the people demand to know all the material facts bearing upon the lives of their leading spirits. Much that a man is is accountable for in his origin. A man is in nowise responsible for his origin. A knowledge of a man's origin is indispensable to a full and correct insight into his character. The nature of a man's origin can not in anywise affect his reputation. Good name is adduced from the acts, the deeds, the life of the man and not from his antecedents. False canons may smother and stultify important truths in the life of a hero, but they can not destroy them. The world is determined that its great shall not be hidden from it. It is eager to gaze upon them in the light of noonday. The world loves to look at the thing as it is, and, in its final judgment, it is just. It has its homage for strength and perfection,

and its charity for weakness and imperfection ;
its emulation for virtue and contempt for vice.

The world has unfading faith in the ability
of the good name and fame of Abraham Lincoln to take care of themselves. It don't want
any Lincoln apocrypha, nor Lincoln apotheo-
sization. It simply wants " Honest Abe" from
the cradle to the grave, and it wants every important truth and fact and incident bearing
upon his character, antecedent and succeed-
ent to his advent in the world, nicely, artless-
ly, justly. But to recur to the subject under
consideration :

It is very remarkable that the biographies
of Messrs. Herndon and Weik, and of Mr. Lamon, written a couple of decades before this
tradition, should have taken note of the identical facts herein recorded, namely, that Mr.
Lincoln was illegitimate and that Abraham
Enloe was his father. At the time of the
writing of their biographies nor at any time
subsequent, so far as is known, did Messrs.
Herndon and Weik and Mr. Lamon know anything of the North Carolina tradition. Not
one of the witnesses for the North Carolina

tradition, at the time the testimony was taken, had ever seen a copy of either edition of these biographies or knew aught of their contents. Another and remarkable thing is that the two leading facts of the North Carolina tradition went from Kentucky to Missouri as early as 1828. The Enloes, Leslies, Simpsons, Shorts and Van Pools of Kentucky and Missouri, of 1824–1835, were familiar with the facts. Everywhere the gossip was the same, that Abraham Lincoln was the son of Abraham Enloe—in New York, Missouri, Mississippi, Florida, North Carolina, Kentucky—and long before a biography of Mr. Lincoln was dreamed of—before the war and during the war and after the war.

It is remarkable that the only ante-bellum biographer of Mr. Lincoln, the only biographer who is accredited with having got his data from Mr. Lincoln's own lips, and who enjoyed the honor of having his proofs read by Mr. Lincoln, obtained from Mr. Lincoln a secret about his ancestry which he (Lincoln) did not wish *published then*, and which he (the biographer Mr. John Loake Scripps) died without revealing to any one.

It is remarkable that Mr. Lincoln should disclose the fact that "his mother was the illegitimate daughter of Lucy Hanks and a well-bred Virginia farmer or planter," entering upon an illumined discussion of hereditary traits as between legitimate and illegitimate offspring, and then suddenly draw around himself a barrier of sombre silence, Mr. Herndon was *afraid* to penetrate. Was it the disclosure he had made as to his mother's illegitimacy, or the *next* step in the process of disclosure—his *own* illegitimacy, at which he lapsed? Abraham Lincoln always lapsed into reticence at this point in his discourse where, to his mind, to have continued would have impaired his personal, or the public, final interest. At the time at which he was talking with Mr. Herndon, nor at the time he divulged the secret to Mr. Scripps was it expedient, to his mind, to make this latter matter of public disclosure. It was something he did not wish "published *then*" and relating to his ancestry.

It is remarkable that there could never be

found official record of the marriage of Thomas
Lincoln and Nancy Hanks ; that there should
have been no affection between Thomas Lincoln
and Abraham Lincoln his reputed son ; that
the former should have treated the latter with
great and habitual cruelty ; that there should
have been a sister older than Abraham but no
vestige of proof that he even recognized her
while she lived, or referred to her after her
death—an only sister. It is remarkable that
this sister's name is subject for difference between biographers—some, able and well informed, contending that her name was Nancy,
and others equally able and well informed,
affirming that her name was Sarah. It is remarkable that there should have been any
variance of information among Lincoln biographers as to the given name of the father of
Thomas Lincoln. It is still more remarkable
that the variance is between one biographer,
a down-easter, Dr. Holland, on the one side,
and Thomas Lincoln's own family and life-
time associates, on the other. Dr. Holland
contending without verification that Thomas
Lincoln's father's name was Abraham ; and

on the other hand, the Hankses—John and
Dennis (Dennis here being disinterested), and
Col. Chapman, who married Thomas Lincoln's
stepdaughter, submitting that his name was
Mordecai, and that this Mordecai, Thomas
Lincoln's father, had four brothers—John,
Jacob, Isaac and Thomas.

It is remarkable that, according to the testimony of the family there was not a single
member named Abraham prior to the advent
of the President, and that Dr. Holland should
have discovered the given name of the grand-
sire to be the same as that of the President.
It is remarkable that Abraham has been a
common name among the Enloes for a hundred years. Indeed it is remarkable opposite
this tradition that the child was christened
Abraham.

It is remarkable that the Bible record of
births and deaths which purports to be in the
handwriting of the President devotes so much
space to the Johnsons, who were of no blood
relation, and so little to his mother, reputed
sister, reputed father and the Hankses and
Lincolns, who should have been bound to

him by the most sacred ties of blood and memory.

Finally, it is remarkable, if the tradition that Abraham Enloe was the father of Abraham Lincoln be a fabrication and a fraud, that certain influences of standing and power should have sought with so much diligence and persistency to run it to earth and break or destroy it. Over against the subject of these pages all these facts are very pre-engaging and remarkable.

In connection with this tradition we deem the history of the Enloe family of much importance. It has, however, for obvious reasons, been our first and foremost object to strengthen and perfect the lines of the main fact of this book. But, fortunately, in so doing we have come into possession of quite an interesting and extended account of certain branches of the Enloe family resident in States other than North Carolina. For the majority of this data we are directly indebted to Dr. I. N. Enloe of Jefferson City, Missouri.

It is evident from this and other record that the family is of Scotch origin,—that the originals came from Scotland is borne out by all the testimony.

It is also evident there are two brothers—first settlers—accounted for by informed members of the family residing in different States and unacquainted with each other. These two brothers stopped in York District, South Carolina. They were school teachers by profession. Their names were Isaac and Enoch.

It is further evident that all the Enloes known to this narrative sprang from these two forbears, and that Gilbert Enloe was the son of Isaac. Gilbert Enloe, therefore, could not have been the father of Abraham Enloe, the father of Abraham Lincoln.

James Enloe, of Missouri, a descendant of Enoch, states it as his opinion that Wesley and the other Enloes, of North Carolina, were mistaken as to Gilbert's having been the father of Abraham; and Rev. Asahel Enloe, the son of Gilbert, says that his father was the son of Isaac; that he knew Abraham Enloe and that his father called him "Cousin Abram."

There are no more intelligent people in North Carolina than the Enloes—Abraham's descendants ; they are among the State's foremost citizens, but, like thousands of others, a busy life with some one of its manifold unavoidable circumstances, has prevented their preserving the lines of descent.

Thorough investigation, when we have time, we are confident will disclose the fact that Abraham, the father of Lincoln, was the son of Enoch Enloe, of York District, South Carolina, unless there were three instead of two original brothers who settled there, and Abraham was the son of the unknown one. The weight of evidence, however, is in favor of the theory that only two Scotsmen—Isaac and Enoch—settled in York District. All the North Carolina testimony being the same, that Abraham Enloe came to this State from York District, he must have been the son of one of these old school teachers. The Enloes—sturdy Scotsmen—are one family, representative, self-sustaining, self-respecting, patriotic, intelligent, progressive, of the best American citizenship, and worthy of Abraham Lincoln or any other man.

Through the gracious agency of Mr. John
E. Burton, of Milwaukee, Wisconsin, a Lincoln specialist, and by the generous courtesy
of Mr. Levin C. Handy, we have obtained the
following :

"WASHINGTON, D. C.,
Nov. 26, 1903.

MR. JOHN E. BURTON :

You are authorized to use in print, in a
book now being published by James H. Cathey,
any picture of Abraham Lincoln standing,
sitting or otherwise, as shown by any negative from which prints are made by me.

LEVIN C. HANDY,
Nephew and Successor of
M. B. Brady,
449 Maryland Ave., S. W.,
Washington, D. C."

The charming sitting picture of Mr. Lincoln
was made by Mr. Brady for his private collection, and Mr. Lincoln sat just to suit the artist.

His nephew had never copied it until he
did so for Mr. Burton. Mr. Brady made two
proofs of this rare picture, and then by a misfortune dropped the plate and broke it into

forty pieces. Mr. Brady's nephew has been offered $100.00 for the other proof.

Mr. Brady's nephew gave a rough print of it for public exhibition in the Presbyterian celebration of the 150th anniversary of that church recently held at Washington. The full length, standing likeness of Mr. Lincoln is from the actual, original, glass negative of Mr. Brady.

Mr. Brady took practically all the Lincoln and other official photographs from 1860 to 1895–8.

His nephew, Mr. Handy, is the only heir to all, and sold many of them in a lump to the United States government for $25,000. We, therefore, congratulate the public, through the generosity of Mr. Handy, by way of the goodness of Mr. Burton, upon its great fortune in being permitted to admire these unique specimens of the accomplished artist upon the homely, handsome face and form of Abraham Lincoln, and we trust the student of this tradition will not neglect the physical comparison thereby facilitated.

JAMES H. CATHEY.

Sylva, N. C.

PART II.—TRUTH RECOVERED FROM SUPPRESSED HISTORIC RECORD.

After three years of diligent search the author has come into the temporary possession and use of the suppressed edition of the Life of Abraham Lincoln by William H. Herndon. It is hardly necessary to state that Mr. Herndon, now deceased, was a citizen of Springfield, Illinois, and the intimate, personal friend and law-partner of Mr. Lincoln, and that the partnership which extended over near a quarter of a century, was dissolved by the untimely death of the latter.

The suppressed edition consists of three volumes of six hundred and thirty-eight pages, bound in dark blue cloth, with the facsimile autograph of Mr. Lincoln imprinted in gold upon the back, and the face of Mr. Lincoln, also in gold, upon the backbone of the book. The edition is abundantly illustrated. It is published by Messrs. Belford, Clark & Co.

Mr. Jesse W. Weik was a collaborator upon these volumes and his name so appears in the book. The edition is now rare to the ragged edge of extinction—a set selling for from fifteen to twenty-five dollars.

The edition was suppressed because of some paragraphs therein that were objectionable to certain individuals. These paragraphs are known by a comparison of the original or suppressed edition and the new or current edition, consisting of two volumes bound in green cloth, embracing six hundred and seventy-nine pages, including a lengthy introduction by Mr. Horace White, and published by Messrs. D. Appleton & Co.

A comparative examination of the two editions will show the matter appearing in the old or suppressed, and expurgated in the new or current edition, as follows: Volume 1, pages 3, 4, 5, 6 and 7 — " His (Lincoln's) theory in discussing the matter of hereditary traits had been, that, for certain reasons, illegitimate children are oftentimes sturdier and brighter than those born in lawful wedlock; and in his case, he believed that his better nature and finer qualities came from this broadminded, unknown Virginian. The relation—

painful as it was—called up the recollection
of his mother, and as the buggy jolted over
the road (Mr. Herndon and Mr. Lincoln were
on their way to court), he added : ' God bless
my mother ; all that I am or ever hope to be I
owe to her' ; and immediately lapsed into silence. Our interchange of ideas ceased, and
we rode on for some time without exchanging
a word. He was sad and absorbed. Burying
himself in thought and musing, no doubt,
over the disclosure he had made, he drew
round him a barrier which I feared to penetrate. His words and melancholy tone made
a deep impression on me.

It was an experience I can never forget.
As we neared the town of Petersburg we were
overtaken by an old man, who rode beside us
for awhile and entertained us with reminis-
cences of days on the frontier. Lincoln was
reminded of several Indiana stories, and by
the time we had reached the unpretentious
court house at our destination, his sadness had
passed away.

After Mr. Lincoln had obtained some
prominence in the world, persons who knew

both himself and his father were constantly
pointing to the want of resemblance between
the two. The old gentleman was not only
deprived of energy and shiftless, and because
of these persons were unable to account for
the source of his son's ambition and intellectual superiority over other men. Hence the
charge so often made in Kentucky that Mr.
Lincoln was in reality the offspring of a Hardin or a Marshall, or that he had in his veins
the blood of some of the noted families who
held social and intellectual sway in the western part of the State. These serious hints
were the outgrowth of the campaign of 1860,
which was conducted with such unrelenting
prejudice in Kentucky that in the county
where Lincoln was born only six persons
could be found who had the courage to vote
for him. I remember that after his nomination for the Presidency, Lincoln received from
Kentucky many enquiries about his family
and origin. This curiosity on the part of the
people for one who had attained such prominence was perfectly natural, but it never
pleased him in the least; in fact to one man

who was endeavoring to establish a relationship through the Hanks family he simply
answered : ' You are mistaken about my
mother,' without explaining the mistake or
making further mention of the matter.

Samuel Haycroft, the clerk of the court in
Hardin county, invited him to visit the scenes
of his birth and boyhood, which led him to
say in a letter, June 4, 1860 : ' You suggest
that a visit to the place of my nativity might
be pleasant to me. Indeed it would, but
would it be safe ? Would not the people
lynch me ?'

That reports reflecting on his origin and
descent should arise in a community in which
he felt that his life was unsafe was by no
means surprising.

Regarding the paternity of Lincoln a great
many surmises and a still larger amount of
unwritten or, at least, unpublished, history
have drifted into the currents of western lore
and journalism.

A number of such traditions are extant in
Kentucky and other localities. Mr. Weik has
spent considerable time investigating the

truth of a report current in Bourbon county, Kentucky, *that Thomas Lincoln, for a consideration from one Abraham Inlow, a miller there, assumed the paternity of the infant child of a poor girl named Nancy Hanks; and after marriage removed with her to Washington or Hardin county, where the son, who was named Abraham, after his real, and Lincoln after his putative father, was born.*

A prominent citizen of the town of Mount Sterling, in that State, who was at one time judge of the court and subsequently editor of a newspaper, and who was descended from the Abraham Inlow mentioned, has written a long argument in support of his alleged kinship through this source to Mr. Lincoln. He emphasizes the striking similarity in stature, facial features, and length of arms, notwithstanding the well-established fact that the first-born child of the real Nancy Hanks was not a boy, but a girl; and that the marriage did not take place in Bourbon, but in Washington county.''

* * *

Next to the biography of Mr. Lincoln by

WESLEY M. ENLOE, Age 81.

his law-partner above quoted from, for open method and frank and fearless statement, ranks the life of Mr. Lincoln by Ward H. Lamon. This work consists of one volume, in octavo form, and contains on extra large paper 547 pages, beside 14 pages of introductory matter, and was published by Messrs. James R. Osgood & Co., of Boston.

Mr. Lamon was the man who spirited Mr. Lincoln to his post at Washington when it was thought his life was sought.

Personal fitness and circumstances familiar to the informed student of Abraham Lincoln rendered Mr. Lamon peculiarly competent to write the truthful life of Mr. Lincoln. In addition to his own rare materials he purchased for three thousand dollars the use of the original manuscript of Mr. Herndon. He labored against the hardship of having an unnatural public taboo his book. His book was vigorously attacked, but in the attack attention was called to the fact that Lincoln's biography, summed up, published to the world that "Abraham Lincoln was of illegitimate origin and lived and died an infidel."

This statement aroused inquiry ; people began to search for old copies of Lamon's Lincoln until, at this writing, it is in such demand that a copy sells for from four dollars and fifty cents to twelve dollars at public auction.

This book was also suppressed.

Apropos to the narrative of these pages I quote from this suppressed edition of Lamon's Life of Lincoln as follows :

"His father's name was Thomas Lincoln and his mother's maiden name was Nancy Hanks.

At the time of his birth they are *supposed* to have been married *about three years.*

Although there appears to have been *little sympathy or affection* between Thomas and Abraham Lincoln, *they were nevertheless connected by ties and associations which make the previous history of Thomas Lincoln and his family a necessary part of any reasonably full biography of the great man who immortalized the name by* WEARING IT."

Further : " Dr. Holland says that the father of Thomas Lincoln was named Abraham, but gives no authority for his statement, and is as likely to be wrong as to be right. The Hankses, Dennis and John, who passed a great part of their lives in the company of Thomas Lincoln, tell us that the name of the father of Thomas Lincoln was Mordecai, and so also does Col. Chapman, who married Thomas Lincoln's step-daughter. Dr. Holland says, also, that the father of Thomas Lincoln had four brothers, John, Jacob, Isaac and Thomas."

Further: "Thomas Lincoln (Abraham's father) was comparatively short and stout, standing about five feet ten inches in his shoes. His hair dark, face round and full, complexion brown. He was a vagrant; in politics a Democrat; in religion nothing and everything—a Free Will Baptist in Kentucky, a Presbyterian in Indiana and a Campbellite in Illinois. He was variously called Lincoln, Linckhern and Linckhorn. He was married sometime in 1806 to Nancy Hanks. It is true that Nancy did not live with her uncle. It is admitted by all the old residents of the place that they were honestly married, but precisely *when or where no one can tell.* Diligent and thorough researches by the most competent persons have failed to discover any trace of the fact in the records of Hardin and adjoining counties. The license and the minister's return in the *marriage of Thomas Lincoln and Sarah Johnson, his second wife*, were easily found in the place where the law required them to be, *but of Nancy Hanks' marriage there exists no evidence but that of mutual acknowledgment and cohabitation.*"

Again : " It is not likely that Tom Lincoln cared a straw about his (Abraham's) education. He had none himself and is said to have admired muscle more than mind. Nevertheless, as Abraham's sister was going to school for a few days at a time, he was sent along, as Dennis Hanks remarks, more to bear her company than with any expectation or DESIRE that *he* would *learn much himself.*"

Again : " Being a wanderer by nature he (Thomas Lincoln) began to long for a change. His decision, however, was hastened by certain troubles between him and one Abraham Enlow. These troubles culminated in a desperate combat between the two men. They

fought like savages; but Lincoln obtained a
signal and permanent advantage by biting off
the nose of his antagonist, so that he went
bereft all the days of his life, and published
his audacity and its punishment wherever he
showed his face. But the affray, and the fame
of it, made Lincoln more anxious than ever
to escape from Kentucky. He resolved, therefore, to leave these scenes forever, and seek a
roof-tree beyond the Ohio.

It has pleased some of Mr. Lincoln's biographers to represent this removal of his father
as a flight from the taint of slavery. Nothing
could be further from the truth. There were
not at the time more than fifty slaves in all
Hardin county, which then composed a vast
area of territory. It was practically a free
community. Lincoln's more fortunate relatives in other parts of the State were slave-
holders; and there is not the slightest evidence that he ever disclosed any conscientious
scruples concerning the institution."

Again: "The lives of his father and mother,
and the history and character of the family
before their settlement in Indiana, *were topics*

upon which Mr. Lincoln never spoke but with great reluctance and significant reserve. In his family Bible he kept a register of births, marriages and deaths, every entry being carefully made in his own hand-writing. It contains the date of his sister's birth and his own ; of the marriage and death of his sister ; of the death of his mother ; and of the birth and death of Thomas Lincoln ; the rest of the record is almost wholly devoted to the Johnstons and their numerous descendants and connections. It has not a word about the Hanks or the Sparrows. It shows the marriage of Sally Bush, first with Daniel Johnston, and then with Thomas Lincoln ; *but it is entirely silent as to the marriage of his own mother. It does not even give the date of her birth, but barely recognizes her* EXISTENCE *and demise* to make the vacancy which was speedily filled by Sarah Johnston."

And again : "An artist was painting his portrait and asked him for a sketch of his life. He gave him this brief memorandum : 'I was born February 12, 1809, in Hardin county, Kentucky, at a point within the now county of La Rue, a mile or a mile and a half from where Hodgen's mill now is. My parents being dead and my own memory not serving, I know of no means of identifying the precise locality. It was on Nolin Creek.'"

And again: "To the compiler of the 'Dictionary of Congres' he gave the following: 'Born Feb. 9, 1809, in Hardin county, Kentucky. Education defective. Profession a lawyer. Have been a Captain of Volunteers in the Black-Hawk war. Postmaster at a very small office. Four times a member of the Illinois Legislature, and was a member of the Lower House of Congress.'"

Further: "To a campaign biographer who applied for particulars of his early history, he replied that they could be of no interest. Mr. Lincoln communicated some facts to this biographer about his ancestry which he did not wish published then."

Again: "Life among the Hankses the Lincolns and the Enlows was a long way below life among the Bushes, and Sarah was the proudest of the Bushes."

And again: " We are told by Col. Chapman

that Abe's father, Tom Lincoln, habitually treated him with great barbarity. Mr. Lincoln through life took little notice of his father."

And again : "In the gallery of family portraits painted by Dennis" (Hanks) "every face looks down upon us with the serenity of innocence and virtue. There is no spot on the fame of any of them. No family could have a more vigorous or chivalrous defender than he, or one who repelled with greater scorn any rumor to their discredit. The Enlow story! Dennis almost scorned to confute it; but, when he did get at it, he settled it by a magnificent exercise of invective genius. He knew 'this Abe Enlow' well, he said, and he had been dead precisely fifty-five years. But, whenever the truth can be told without damage to the character of a Lincoln or a Hanks, Dennis will tell it candidly enough, provided there is no temptation to magnify himself. His testimony, however, has been sparingly used throughout these pages; and no statement has been taken from him, unless it was more or less corroborated by some one else. The better part of his evidence Mr. Herndon

Lincoln in Standing Posture, with Allen Pinkerton on his right and Gen. LaFayette C. Baker on his left, heads of Detective Departments.

WESLEY ENLOE

At the Age of 81.   Son of Abraham Enloe.

The most striking similarity between Mr. Lincoln and Wesley Enloe is their physical formation and characteristics, which may be seen from the above comparative standing likeness.

took the precaution of reading carefully to John Hanks, who pronounced it substantially true; and that circumstance gives it undeniable value."

I quote from " Horton's Youth's History of the Great Civil War." Mr. Horton was a citizen of New York. In his biographical sketch of Abraham Lincon, among other things, he says:

· " He had the misfortune not to know who his father was; and his mother, alas, was a person to reflect no honor upon her child. Launched into the world an outcast, and started on the road of being without parental care, and without the advantage of even a common-school education, he certainly was entitled to great credit for gaining even the limited mental culture which he possessed. He ran away from his wretched home at the age of nine, to escape the brutal treatment of the man who had married his mother and was forced to get his bread by working on a flat-boat on the Mississippi."

In the preface to the first volume of his biography Mr. Herndon says : "With a view to throwing a light upon some attributes of Lincoln's character heretofore obscure, and thus contributing to the great fund of history these volumes are given to the world.

It is alike just to his memory and the proper legacy of mankind that the whole truth concerning him should be known.

If the story of his life is truthfully and courageously told—nothing colored or suppressed ; nothing false either written or suggested—the reader will see and feel the real presence of the man.

If, on the other hand, the story is colored or the facts in any degree suppressed, the reader will be not only misled, but imposed upon as well.

At last the truth will come and no man need hope to evade it.

Lincoln's character, I am certain will bear close scrutiny. I am not afraid of you in this direction. Don't let anything deter you fiom digging to the bottom. In drawing the portrait tell the world what the skeleton was with Lincoln. What gave him that peculiar mel-

ancholy. What cancer had he inside. Espe-
cial attention is given to the history of his
youth and early manhood; and while dwelling
on this portion of his life the liberty is taken
to insert many things that would be *omited* or
suppressed in other places where the cast-iron
rules that govern magazine writing prevail.
Mr. Lincoln was my warm, devoted friend. I
always loved him, and revere his name to this
day. My purpose to tell the truth about him
need occasion no apprehension; for I know
that God's naked truth, as Carlyle puts it, can
never injure the fame of Abraham Lincoln.

Some persons will doubtless object to the
narrative of certain facts which appear here
for the first time, and which they contend
should be consigned to the tomb. Their pre-
tense is that no good can come from such
ghastly exposures. To such over-sensitive
souls, if any such exist, my answer is that
these facts are indispensable to a full knowledge of Mr. Lincoln in all the walks of life."

The forgoing is Mr. Herndon's apology for
writing his faithful life of Abraham Lincoln.
He says he loved Mr. Lincoln and revered his

name. Moreover he says he was the personal depository of the larger part of the most valuable Lincolniana in existence.

Hear what no less authority than Mr. Horace White says of Mr. Herndon's peculiar qualifications for the task of writing a true characterization of Abraham Lincoln : " What Mr. Lincoln was after he became President can be best understood by knowing what he was before. The world owes more to William H. Herndon for this particular knowledge than to all other persons taken together. It is no exaggeration to say that his death removed from earth the person who, of all others, had most thoroughly searched the sources of Mr. Lincoln's biography and had most attentively, and also lovingly, studied his character. He was nine years the junior of Mr. Lincoln. Their partnership began in 1843 and it continued until it was dissolved by the death of the senior member. Between them there was never an unkind word or thought.

As a portraiture of the man Lincoln—and this is what we look for above all things else in a biography—I venture to think that Mr. Herndon's work will never be surpassed."

PART III.—FURTHER FOLK-LORE.

I quote from a letter received from Rev. S. E. Kennedy, of Davis, Indian Territory, of date July 7, 1898.

The Davis Weekly News, of his home town, says of him : " Rev. S. E. Kennedy is pastor of the Christian Church here, and is loved and esteemed universally by all who have the pleasure of knowing him. He wrote :

" 'My grandfather and grandmother, John and Fannie Kennedy, lived neighbor to Abraham Enloe in North Carolina, and were well acquainted with both Abraham Enloe and Nancy Hanks. My grandmother was born about 1775. Her story of the Enloe-Hanks embroglio was substantially as follows : ' The father of Nancy Hanks was a drunkard and was so cruel to his wife and children that he was imprisoned and made to make shoes as a punishment. The mother of Nancy Hanks was forced because of her inability to support them to bind her children out. Abraham Enloe took Nancy, and a man by the name

of Pratt took Mandy. Mr. and Mrs. Pratt
were kind to Mandy and taught her to card
and spin and weave. Mandy did well and
married Samuel Henson and moved across
the mountains. Abraham Enloe became entangled with Nancy and caused her to be
taken to Kentucky and to be married to Tom
Lincoln, who kept a stillhouse there. Abraham Enloe promised to give Tom Lincoln
five hundred dollars, a wagon and pair of
mules if he would marry Nancy Hanks, but
after Lincoln had got drunk and attempted to
kill Abraham Enloe, they compromised, and
Enloe gave Lincoln a mule, a mare and fifteen
dollars in money, whereupon Lincoln took
Nancy and little Abe back to Kentucky, and
I never saw them more.' "

Mr. Kennedy says : "My grandmother lived
to be near ninety, dying about the year 1866.
She could neither read nor write, but possessed the most perfect memory I have ever
observed. She knew Abraham Enloe before
and after they moved across the mountains.
Whether my grandparents came with Enloe
when he migrated to North Carolina, I do not

know. What was meant by 'across the mountains' I have forgotten, if I ever knew.

"My father and mother moved to Wetumpka, Alabama, in the early 40's. I was born at Wetumpka. Not long after the removal of my parents to Wetumpka one of the Enloes also moved from the old North Carolina home, and settled two miles east of Wetumpka. He raised a large family. He is dead, but the family still reside there."

I quote from a letter of Mr. James D. Enloe of date May 17, 1899. Mr. Enloe's address is Cedartown, Georgia. He wrote: "During the war, while I was around Petersburg, Va., I was reading the Richmond *Dispatch* and ran across a communication by John L. Hellem. Hellem was my father's sister's son. The article stated that Abraham Lincoln was the illegitimate son of Abraham Enloe, an uncle of mine. If he wrote the truth you must be mistaken. But you may be right. My grandfather was named Abraham Enloe and came from either North Carolina or South Carolina and settled on Nolen Creek,

Hardin County, Kentucky. Nancy Hanks married Lincoln in that county. I was personally acquainted with Lincoln. I am now in my seventy-sixth year."

I quote from a letter from Doctor Thomas H. Hammond of date July 19, 1899. Dr. Hammond then resided in Wildwood, Florida. He wrote : '' When I was in Camp Wickliff, Ky., in January, 1862, I heard Lieut.-Col. Wilder, of the 17th Indiana Regiment, say that Abraham Lincoln was an illegitimate. Col. Wilder was a very important man with Gen. William Nelson ; going over the country giving Gen. Nelson information about the roads, bridges, etc., and he was over the country where Lincoln had lived. In December, 1878, I went to Kansas and remained in that State for six years. While there a Baptist preacher, who hailed from Kentucky, asked me if I knew that Lincoln was an illegitimate. I told him I had heard it. In 1884 I came to Florida. Professor Borden was in the Confederate Army, and in that country . (in Kentucky where Lincoln was born) during

the war. He had heard that Lincoln was an
illegitimate, and related facts that aroused my
interest and curiosity. The Baptist preacher
above mentioned, meantime, had come to
Florida, but had gone to Taylorsville, Kentucky. I wrote to him asking him who the
reputed father of Abraham Lincoln was. He
did not know himself, coming from a different part of the State, but his wife and mother
did ; his father was Abraham Inlow."

I quote from a letter of Mr. Nat R. Ander-
son, of Rolling Fork, Mississippi, of date May
28, 1899. He wrote : " I am a native of the
Shenandoah Valley in Virginia, Rocking-
ham county. That State is where the Lincolns
sprang from. Tom Lincoln's father migrated
from there to Kentucky. Many of them are
still there. They pronounced the name there
Link-horn. I never could understand how so
great and good a man as " Old Abe " could
have descended from such a low breed and
entirely worthless a vagabond as Tom Lincoln. I have read most of the lives of Lincoln.
The best were by Ward H. Lamon and W. H.

Herndon, his law-partner, but these were suppressed.

I am now an old man past three score and ten. I remember most of the stirring events since Jackson's second term; all the leading men and measures, and notwithstanding our difference in party affiliation, I frankly confess that no man has interested me more, from his strange, eventful and lowly life, than Abraham Lincoln.

You are undoubtedly due the thanks of every lover of truth and respectability in the land in finding for the immortal Railsplitter an honorable paternity and strong and well-defined ancestry."

The following is extracted from a letter received from G. J. Davie, of Nevada, Texas, bearing date May 5, 1899: "I was raised on the border of Christian county, Kentucky, on the Tennessee side. I knew many of the Enloes and have all my life known that Lincoln was the son of old Abe Enloe.

I was educated at the University of North Carolina, class of '52."

Following is the full text of a letter of Judge James Shaw upon his perusal of a copy of the first edition of this Genesis :

MOUNT CARROLL, ILL., March 19, 1900.

"My Dear Mr. Cathey:

" Your little book was duly received. I have read and re-read it with *deep interest. I always knew there was a mystery about the early life of Lincoln,* but did not know very well what it was. Your book gives me to understand many things I have seen and heard about this wonderful man.

The address I have been giving a few times in this part of Illinois is only partly in type. It is mostly an oral address. When I was a boy and later a young man Lincoln practiced law in the courts of Cass county where my father lived. I attended them a good deal. Heard him try the Armstrong murder case at Beardstown, and was present when the jury brought in their verdict of acquittal, and witnessed the memorable scene which then took place. He was often at my father's house in those days. Later when I spent five years at Illinois College, Jacksonville, Ill., he came often to the courts there, and I made a habit of attending the trials in that county ; I also used to be about his office in Springfield a good deal when he was in full practice there. The man had a wonderful fasciuation for me, and took some pains to advise me in preparing myself to become a lawyer. His strange, weird, sad face ; his wonderful personality, made a lasting impression on me. In my address I have simply talked about him from my personal recollections and from close observation of the man during his rise to greatness. I am full of the subject and have interested our people up here a good deal with these personal recollections, and descriptions of the man and his mental and physical characteristics.

I would be pleased to hear from you at any time as to anything in the line you are working up so interestingly.

Very truly yours,

JAMES SHAW."

Rev. Asahel Enloe was for a short while a resident of Murphy, N. C. Since the date of his letter both he and his son with whom he lived have moved from the State, and it is the writer's information that the old gentleman is dead. His son's whereabouts cannot be now located. The writer enjoyed a very brief acquaintance with Rev. Mr. Enloe while he resided in Murphy. He was not tall of stature, but possessed of the proverbially large Enloe nose and ears. In facial form particularly from a profile view, was the almost exact counterpart of the similar view of Abraham Lincoln. His features were homely but strangely pleasant and prepossessing. He was a gentleman—educated, refined, but familiar as one's grandmother. There was a twinkle of humor about the eye (then blind), and a bubble of homely mirth burst ever and anon in the stream of his conversation. I have often deeply deplored my inability to have known more of him personally.

I am resolved to procure for a subsequent edition of this genesis a portrait of him for further illustration of the theory of this volume, if there be one in existence and to be had. Following is the answers to questions in an interview which I had with him :

My age is 81. My father was named Gilbert. My grandfather was named Isaac. My father had two brothers, Asahel and Nathaniel. Father and uncle Nathaniel lived and died in York District, South Carolina. They were school teachers. Uncle Asahel moved to Southern Illinois. My profession is Presbyterian minister—preaching since 1851. I never held any political office. I graduated at Davidson College, N. C., in 1847, also attended Theological Seminary at Columbia, South Carolina. Most prominent characteristics physically of the Enloes are big ears and long noses. My father and Uncle Asahel were teachers.

My grandfather was a soldier in the Revolutionary war ; was wounded at Hook's defeat, rendering him unfit for further service during war in army. My father was justice of the peace for many years. My oldest brother, Isaac, was a lawyer and practiced his profession in Mississippi ; he was delegate to two

Democratic conventions. My brother John
held office of circuit court clerk in York District, S. C., for several terms.

I first knew Abraham Enloe (alleged father
of Lincoln) about 1827. I knew him well, also
three of his sons—Aseph, Alfred and Scroup.
His sons were all tall, slender and muscular.

Alfred learned the blacksmith trade at my
father's and was a pleasant man—full of good
humor. Can't tell our relation. My father
called him "cousin Abram." He was a
trader in horses, etc., and in his yearly visits
South always visited my father. It was related of him by a Mr. Kennedy, a kinsman,
that if he had every dollar but one and knew
that by riding across the continent he could
get that one, he would make the trip. He
loved to practice jokes and to laugh at their
results. He was about six feet in height.
Never heard of the tradition until after Lincoln was nominated for the Presidency when
I heard the rumor that Lincoln's father was
named Enloe—I was then in Mississippi.

ASAHEL ENLOE.

Murphy, N. C., May 15, 1899.

Following is undoubtedly one of the best if not the best pen portrait of Abraham Lincoln in existence.

It is by Professor Frank M. Vancil who was, at the writing of this letter (this to the writer), Superintendent of the State University Preparatory High School at Lewistown, Montana.

Prof. Vancil was born and reared to manhood in the same neighborhood with Mr. Lincoln in Illinois, was intimately acquainted with him. This physical description Prof. Vancil was so generous as to transcribe from the manuscript of his school history of the United States which he was then engaged in writing:

" He was six feet and four inches in height, the length of his legs being out of all proportion to his body. When he sat on a chair he seemed no taller than the average man, measuring from the chair to the crown of his head but his knees were high in front. He weighed about 180 pounds, but was thin through the breast and had the general appearance of a consumptive. Standing he stooped slightly forward, and sitting he usually crossed his long legs or threw them over the arms of the chair. His head was long and tall from the base of the brain and the eyebrow; his forehead high and narrow, inclining backward as it rose. His ears were very large and stood out; eyebrows heavy, jutting forward over small, sunken, blue eyes; nose large, long, slightly Roman and blunt; chin projecting far and sharp, curved upward to meet a thick lower lip which hung downward; cheeks flabby and sunken, the loose skin falling in folds, a mole on one cheek, and an uncommonly large Adam's apple in his throat. His hair was dark brown, stiff and unkempt; complexion dark, skin yellow, shriveled and leathery. Every feature of the man—the hollow eyes with the dark rings beneath; the long, sallow, cadaverous face, his whole air and walk showed that he was a man of sorrow."

Extract from letter of Prof. Frank M. Vancil, of Lewistown, Mont., of date July 16, 1899.

PART IV.—THE BURTON ORATION.

AUTHOR'S INTRODUCTION TO MR. BURTON'S ORATION.

The fame of "The True Genesis of Abraham Lincoln" having gone to that beautiful Northwestern villa-on-the-lakes—Lake Geneva, Wisconsin, it came under the eye of Mr. John E. Burton, a successful financier and man of letters, residing there. The subject-matter of the little volume at once engaged his serious attention. It had once again fallen under the eye of a peculiarly qualified critic. It had invited the frank and fearless scrutiny of, peradventure, the best informed student of Abraham Lincoln living. Mr. Burton, as he says in his oration, had seen Abraham Lincoln and heard his voice. He is and has always been a steadfast believer in all of the principles and doctrines of which Mr. Lincoln was the exponent. He has always been that which Mr. Lincoln, in the years which led up to the war and even until the end of that dread crisis was in sight, from policy was not,

JOHN E. BURTON.

an ultra-abolitionist. There has not grown
up a citizen of the Republic that is a more
loyal Union man. There is no more devoted
friend of the broken hero of the armies of the
North than he, and the Grand Army of the
Republic whose reunions he has more than
once enjoyed the honor of addressing, has in
him a substantial support. But, Mr. Burton,
in all that is included in the terms man and
citizen, finds his ideal in Abraham Lincoln.
In this conception he is cheerfully joined by
the majority of his contemporaries in the
North, by many of every section of the Republic, and by not a few in every land under the
sun. And he is not a blind hero-worshiper.

As above mentioned, he is familiar with his
hero. There may be other men as well informed upon particular epochs or phases of
Abraham Lincoln's life, but we fearlessly assert
that there is not a man living who is as full of
all that pertains to him—as versatile in the
wide domain of Lincolniana, as is he. He is
the possessor of the rarest, if not the largest,
private collection of works of biography alone
upon Lincoln in existence, the nnmber of vol-

umes now being quite in advance of one
thousand. His portraits, paintings, photographs; his autographs, mementoes and
unique and costly souvenirs, are by the score
and hundred. This rare collection, it is need-
less to say, represents much means and pains,
and his unmatched store of knowledge is the
result of many years of penetrative study
aided by the finest lights, and all combined are
the product of the labor of love.

After reading the first edition of these pages,
Mr. Burton, being convinced of the truth of
the theory therein promulgated, opened a correspondence with the writer that is now
ripened into personal friendship. He ordered
one hundred and fifty copies for circulation
among his friends of the Northwest and gave
the book his unstinted endorsement. He
dived into his deep-sea Lincoln treasure and
brought up the *suppressed* three-volume Life
of the President by his old-time friend and
law partner. He rummaged the musty tomes
of a more recent alcove and hauled forth the
one-volume Life, by Ward Hill Lamon, smoth-
ered in infancy by aristocratic interdict. These

he at once expressed to the writer that the truths that have been temporarily consigned to a quasi-oblivion might be vouchsafed popular access in the light of day. For the above and other valuable Lincolniana, as well as for much highly esteemed information by correspondence, we acknowledge unrequited but grateful indebtedness to Mr. Burton, but especially are we his debtor for the oration which follows.

It has been our inestimable fortune to read most of the great eulogies, characterizations and pen portraits of Abraham Lincoln. The standard are those by Emerson, Ingersoll and Watterson. These three are esteemed classics in the range of eulogistic Lincolniana. Like all , the work of these three gentlemen, they are finished—every stone is hewn without a jar and laid in its exact place without a flaw, but *their structures* are rather fantastic than substantial in effect.

The oration of Mr. Burton is not so much the production of a skilled craftsman who had had his task assigned by assumed public consensus, as it is the product of the self-appointed

duty of the thoroughly equipped laboier in
the vineyard of usefulness. Neither Emerson,
Ingersoll nor Watterson has evinced the close
familiarity with the minutest detail of Abraham Lincoln's entire career that Mr. Burton
evinces in this oration, nor have either treated
that career in a manner nearly so heart-thrilling
and practical. It is true the utterance from
beginning to end shows the author to be of
the ultra class of Lincoln admirers, but this
tendency does not neutralize the salutary effect
of the general estimate. The oration as a
whole is unexampled as a fidelic echo of the
popular estimate of Abraham Lincoln. It is
particularly the truest voicing of the public
mind and heart of the North toward Abraham
Lincoln that has yet been articulated. It pos-
sesses in an eminent degree the element that
will insure popularity—the element of simplicity—plain, primal ideas clothed in terse
and telling Saxon. This was the means employed by Mr. Lincoln himself in reaching the
popular heart. It is sweeping yet detailed;
prophetic yet practical; imaginative yet true.
It is terse, ornate, eloquent; critical, reminis-

cent and profound. His entire portrayal is one of exceptional vividness and power—the outlines are strong, well sustained and faithful, and then each minor feature is brought out with the touch of a master—a man conversant with his theme. Suddenly and without warning you laugh, or cry, or muse as you traverse the way made immortal by his footsteps. It will live as long as men speak the language of liberty and union, of gratitude and love :—

ABRAHAM LINCOLN.

AN ORATION, BY JOHN E. BURTON, OF LAKE GENEVA, WIS.

The character of Abraham Lincoln stands so high above all possible wrong-doing that honesty was never mentioned or thought of as a *virtue* in him.

He was not only the best product of pure American civilization which his century produced, but he was, all in all, the best public man and sincerest statesman who has ever figured in the destiny of this nation or in the history of the world.

To all right-minded Americans he is the ripe and rounded product of *what every man would like to be*, and he will therefore remain, through all time, the symbol of perfected character. The whole world loves Lincoln because he did what the world knows was right, and he avoided doing what the world knows to be wrong, and it is therefore doubtful if any human being will ever again hold a similar position of greatness in a similar and transcendent epoch, or ever fulfill the world's expectations so completely, as did Lincoln.

His fame grows so steadily, so perfectly, so naturally, and so mightily, and the very fiber of his character comes out so brilliantly as the search-light of time reveals him from every possible point of view that the fear among thoughtful men is, that, with the lapse of centuries, his fame may pass the boundary line allotted to flesh and blood and become obscured by entering the realm of the mythical, where he may be lost to the world of struggling men among the gods and the myths which always inhabit the past.

He was the child of Love before he was the

child of Law. Born, not only in poverty, but surrounded by want and suffering ; favored in nothing; wanting in everything which makes up the joys of life, he trudged, as a child, the trail of sorrow, and was the playmate of Grief, and always above and around his mysterious young life there hung the shadow of a dark and mystic cloud.

It was a literal truth that "he had not where to lay his head," and while he did not eat the "locust and wild honey," and while his raiment was not of "camel's hair," yet his clothing was, almost exclusively, "the skin of wild beasts," from his buckskin pants to the ponderous coon skin cap. A meaner or darker origin cannot well be imagined. Not one ray of genuine hope can be discovered to light his childhood. Nature seems to have bruised and hurt him so that in manhood he might gird himself to bind up the wounds of a bleeding nation. She seems to have handicapped and loaded his patient soul that he might justly hate the oppressors of men in his loftiest estate. She seems to have starved him that he might the better feel the hunger and the yearnings of a downtrodden race. His eyes were allowed to look at the sunlight through the greased paper windows of the primitive hut and log school house, that he might, in his conquering prime, appreciate the glory of the noonday sun of universal freedom. Nature was his Mother, his Teacher, his playmate, his All, and with a yearning that was never satiate he grew in stature among the grand old trees of the forest ever surrounded by bird song, flower and fern, and with unsandled feet he walked the rough trail of the pioneer boy straight through over rock and glen to the mountain top of perfect Sincerity, and as a man stood as natural as a child, yet possessed all the powers and knowledge of his sex and his race in their fullness and purity. Almost without playmates, he was the companion of unadorned Nature, and *with the intuition of the child of Nature*, his heart expanded to the influence of the flight of fowl, the basking fish, the habits of the timid deer, the ways of the wild turkey, and bounded with joy in the season of bloom of the wild crab and the

sumach, and resting lazily in the autumn
and Indian summer among the ripening nuts
and the purpling grape, he studied with joy
strange and profound the wondrous move-
ments of planet, moon and star. With a
growth exceeding six feet and four inches
he found himself almost like one awakening
from a dream, a giant in stature with mus-
cles of iron made memorable by felling the
tree and splitting the rail for sturdy use.

Thus he matured, like a prophet of old,
and kept ever close to the great heart of nature. As a matured man he could not sleep
when the storm had blown the nest and the
nestlings from the tree until he had restored
them to the mother bird, and could not rest
in the prime of his matchless manhood until
a race of four millions of fathers, mothers
and children were restored to their natural
rights after the thunder storm of war had
passed, and if we do not anchor his mortal
memory to the ocean bed of solid fact and
history, I fear the day will yet come when
some wild burst in the ruffled flow of human
turmoil will claim him as a Christ. Scarcely an

attribute of the divine character is wanting
in this unique man, who, in all the loneliness
of his early life, was unconsciously schooled,
trained, perfected and graduated in all that
was honest, natural, capable and kind. As a
flat-boatman in the city of New Orleans he
saw, for the first time, negro boys and girls
and young women put up and sold as chattels
upon the auction block, and then and there
the mordant sunk deep into his very soul, and
he said to his companion, "*That's wrong, and
if ever I get a chance to hit it, by God, I'll hit
it hard.*" The "painted lizard" of human
slavery had been photographed forever on his
mind and memory, and he bided his time
with the patience of a God until the day
should come and until the hour had struck
when, with a single blow, he could make good
that oath, and so, later in life, we see him,
amid the billows and blood of war, as he
calmly says, "Wait and see the salvation of
God"—and so it is that *the human race is
waiting to see*, as the years go by, the salvation of eternal right forever triumphant over
wrong and *made possible by his patience and
perfect humanity.*

His patience, however, did not weaken him or class him as quiescent, for when imposed upon and crowded toward insult or cowardice, or if his cause, when justly stated, was assailed by injustice or brutality the sleeping lion showed his fangs and his giant wrath seldom found any bully rash enough to stand in his way when he accepted a challenge. His powerful exhibition when forced by taunt to twice throw the champion Needham at Wabash Point; his righteous rage at New Salem when the leader of the bullies of Clary's Grove, Jack Armstrong, tried by foul means, to get the advantage over him, and again when his excited men in the Black Hawk War attempted to kill the friendly Indian, defying practically the brawn and muscle of the whole regiment, all prove his practical manliness, if occasion demanded, and such was his physical prowess that few men in all that Western country ever wished to dispute his standing.

The great dream of the centuries seems to have blossomed in his eventful life, and the more we learn of it the more we come to realize and to know that in him was the Perfect Man in the sanest and soundest sense of the word, physically, mentally and morally. Poverty made him good ; suffering made him great ; circumstances made him President ; fidelity made him beloved ; courage made him heroic and martyrdom made him immortal.

You may search the minutest records of recorded time and you cannot find another character who made so few mistakes during the chaos of such trying ordeals, or who possessed on all great occasions that sublimity of faith and courage in action, as mark and make the character of Abraham Lincoln ; neither could you find another man who could control, and even guide to glory, all his impetuous subordinates in the heat of conflict and yet without offence compel them to unconscious obedience in the fulfillment of a destiny which he alone could read in the dusk of deathless performance.

The record of this world does not show another character who was *schooled in almost continuous failure in youth and early manhood*, in order that he might the better serve as the successful and great commander in the most momentous epoch of human progress.

No where in the library of nations can you find another character so varied in all experiences, and yet where every experience was clearly given for the perfect formation of a character unique and matchless. Look back over forty years and see a boy ever obedient, even where obedience was not especially commendable, yet *always* obedient; as a son, wise, thoughtful and obliging; as a pupil almost a prodigy, and with a burning zeal for useful knowledge beyond all precedent; as a boatman, capable of utilizing the rough experience of the Mississippi river; as a soldier in the Black Hawk War, little better than a failure because his heart was too big to exercise the cruelties of Indian warfare; as a lover, sincere, poetic and ideal, almost to the border line of insanity; as a debater, candid, clear, original, truthful; as a lawyer, honorable, just, logical; as a writer, fair, witty, useful; as a candidate, weak, but earnest and ever conscious of his superiority; as an antagonist, formidable, real, full of surprises and dangerous; as a victor, modest, gracious and benevolent; as a man, possibly crafty, for a good purpose, but always natural, frank and winning and always commanding and conscious of his higher qualifications; as a leader, slow, always preparing, always aware of the gravity of the situation, action well-timed, and always sustained ; as a patriot, ambitious, but an ambition that never crowded or even approached the limit of his patriotism, therefore absolutely safe in all emergencies ; as a martyr, beautiful beyond that of saint or scientist, and as a memory his was and is the dearest, the gentlest and most God-like.

I have seen Abraham Lincoln and heard his voice. This is to me a happy recollection. From my childhood to this hour I have always kept every printed word which has fallen from his lips. It is the literary pride of my life that I have preserved with loving care all the books, works, biographies, and printed souvenirs of *this real man* of men, until now I shall soon pass the 1,000-volume line and still know that the future is growing with new works perennially. With

other men it was literary achievement; the
triumphs of war; the aggrandizement of con-
quest; the glory of new discovery, or the
flight of imagination in the kingdom of art or
song; but with Lincoln it was character,
character, CHARACTER. This is why his name
grows with each succeeding year. This is
why our American schools, as well as the
schools in foreign lands, are making the 12th
day of February a green spot in the dusty
road of school routine, and are telling to the
millions of boys and girls the story of a true
patriot, a pure man, a character beyond reproach, the safest model of citizenship, the
Agamemnon of moral power throughout the
world.

It is the pride of millions of men and women to be able to say, "*I have seen Abraham
Lincoln and heard his voice.*" Time will en-
hance the value of everything he ever touched
and hallow his every word. No other character is known to the children of men who was
more bashful or tenderly sensitive to direct
compliment. No man ever feared praise more
than he, and no man ever possessed a su-

premer contempt or indifference to unjust criticism or slander, and no man ever lived who was more conscious of his own actual worth and his ability to use that worth for the good of others. No man at his death was ever so universally or so sincerely mourned, as Lincoln. The world wept as a young child at its father's bier. His funeral train was fourteen hundred miles long and his mourners moistened with sincerity's tears the soil of every civilized land, while official history required nine hundred and thirty pages to print the plain record of telegram, resolution and sorrow of the nations.

He was not really an orator, as the world goes, yet his speech on the battlefield of Gettysburg, his inaugural address are terse and treasured classics and ranks with any sayings that time has preserved from the lips or pen of Cicero, Pericles, Phillip or Phocian. No orator ever touched the tender cords which sweep the heartstrings in the soul of womanhood more deftly than he when he said, while pleading the case of the widow of the old soldier of 1812 : ''Time rolls on. The heroes of 1776 have passed away and are encamped on the other shore. *The old soldier has gone to his rest.—Crippled, blinded and broken, his widow comes to me and to you, gentlemen of the jury, to right her wrongs. She was not always thus. She was once beautiful as the morning. Her step was as light, her face as fair and her voice as sweet as ever rung in the lanes of old Virginia. Now she is poor, defenseless. Shall we, too, cast her off?"* His courtroom was in tears. His suit was won.

No man ever held woman in higher esteem than Abraham Lincoln, and woman to-day is his loyal lover and defence, through ill and good report, and through her there shall be engravened the ideal Lincoln in the minds of millions yet unborn.

If all men could be like Lincoln there would be no need of heaven. His pattern was formed in the Foundry of Fate, and when the world's greatest epoch had closed the mould was found to fit "the head of the corner." See his tall form sway under a sorrow almost infinite as he stands at the coffin of his dead benefactor, Bowlin Greene, and although a man of thirty-three, his heart breaks with uncontrolled emotion as he tries to speak the words of gratitude and tender eulogy which he longed to express, but in the agony of his soul's despair he fails to make a sound, and, in a burst of overwhelming tears and groans, he leaves the scene. Never did a human heart offer to the dead a truer tribute. Language can never tell the depth of his feelings and history will never record a wail more tender or a lay more sweet and divine.

When the tender life of his first pure love went out and Ann Rutledge was laid in her grave; his was the pathetic voice which, in poignant grief, cried aloud as his vanishing reason all but left him : "*I can never let the rains, the snow and the storms beat upon her grave!*" A deeper anguish never pierced the heart of an honest man since Christ wept in Gethsemane.

Oh, what a legacy, what a heritage for us and ours and our heirs forever after us, and for the world, as Time, the Saviour reveals his growing worth ! Oh, the great, broad,

patient, courageous man, so calm in the tem-
pest that radicals could not rush him and the
trumpet of war could not intimidate him!
His was the courage of the sublimest order;
absolutely perfect in faith and that faith
founded upon eternal justice and upon his
perfect trust in a God of justice, and in his
own people and upon his own true and righteous self. You have but to put your ear to
the welded rail of the past and the echoes of
forty years will come back to you, and above
the din and confusion of that awful period you
will hear the clear, patriotic voice of a nation
and that triumphant song,

"*We are coming, Father Abraham, three hundred
thousand more.*"

This mighty surge of song is not the wail
of despair nor the measured tone of defiance,
but the belated and mighty response of thirty
millions of patriots sounding the cry which
comes from the deep, welling passion of
patriotism, echoing across plain and river,
and over hill and mountain top, that a million
defenders invincible as an army with banners
were coming in response to his righteous call

to save from dissolution and death *the one na-tion which was and is, and is to be*, the hope of the world.

How strange it all seems to us now! The world will always see him, in the National storm of passion and the flow of fraternal blood, *a moral hero*, and in the blast that blinded, he held the helm of State for four dark and terrible years, and until Fate had become fulfillment, and then in the sunshine of peace he appeared in the Capital of Rebel-lion like a closing tableau, holding the trust-ing hand of his innocent boy while the fren-zied negro bows in almost idolatrous worship at his feet, and then he is suddenly lifted, as by some design of fatality, to the realm of earthly immortality. It verily seems as if Fate did play with dates and events, for on the anni-versary of the very day when the starry flag of Ft. Sumter bowed to the bellowing guns of Beauregard four years before, Beecher and his compatriots restored it, in the harbor of Charles-ton, to the breeze of Heaven, and yet before its folds had fairly caught the joyous inspira-tion and while darkness settled upon the land that night his life went out by the hand of the assassin.

No man is ever seen so tenderly as when humanity beholds him through the mellow vail of suffering and undeserved adversity. It is then we realize the force of the sentiment that,

> "Chords that vibrate sweetest music,
> Sound the deepest notes of woe."

It can never be said that religious fanaticism aided him essentially in the completion of his world task; neither that personal ambition rallied him to sudden success, and although success was his ruling motive, and was, all in all, and through it all, his guiding star, yet that success was grounded upon the solid rock of truth, and through the darkness of that wildest and most tempestuous night of sorrow and suffering he stood, the central figure looking over and above the heads of his contemporaries, like the giant he was, surveying the end and seeing the triumphant vision which was to mark the closing of the most remarkable conflict which ever sanctified the battleground of nations.

It is true that there have been other patriots in other lands than ours, and it is true that patriotism has lived as a principle in all the ages of the past, and that there has existed the calm of dignity and the conciousness of power all through the centuries, *but there has · never been but one Lincoln.*

Other men have been earnest and other men have been great, and even sincere, and what is still more, have been kind and useful to their fellow men and have helped to grace and crown the ages, and yet, *I say, there has never been but one Lincoln.*

He did not believe in Christ but he did believe in a God of Justice, in a God that could not tolerate human slavery or injustice among his human kind. He had lived to learn and to know that his own judgment of men was reliable and right, and hence he gradually, but easily and certainly, overshadowed all his associates and contemporaries, and as a character, stands alone from his rough-hewn cradle to his marbled-tomb. 'In all that eventful journey he knew his own ability rightly and neither over-estimated it nor under-estimated it, and he dared to assume dangerous posts of duty, and yet never flinched or doubted. He was therefore greater than the greatest man of his time. He is the Agamemnon of history.

No other man in history seems ever to have centered and focused universal interest in his every and minutest acts and personal characteristics like Lincoln. When standing he towered above his famous opponent, Douglas, fourteen inches, but when both were seated side by side he was but four inches higher, so exceptional were his legs and arms in length compared with his body.

In the Illinois Legislature he belonged to the famous "Long Nine," the name applied to the nine members from his section, of which he was the tallest. and was called the "Sangamon Chief," their combined hight being fifty-five feet. To them and to him were due the success of changing the State Capital from Vandalia to Springfield, Sangamon county, in 1837.

It is remarkable how many men afterward famous were associated with Lincoln during

his early or active life, including Peter Cartwright, famous preacher; Colonel Ellsworth,
first to fall in war; Colonel Baker, hero who
fell at Ball's Bluff; Stephen A. Douglas, patriot
and opponent; Senator Lyman Trumbull,
Governor Bissell, General John A. McClernand,
Judge David Davis and others.

He was born close to the famous Mason and
Dixon's Line, about 39° 33′ north latitude,
marking the line limit of slavery and hence
naturally conservative as to Northern and
Southern opinions.

He was not wholly free from the local super-
stitions of the Kentucky pioneer times, and
the quick and living secrets of nature, while
real and understood, still carried a tinge of the
marvellous, for night winds, dark forests,
swelling streams, cries of wild beasts, sudden
deaths, moaning trees, and avenging storms,
sometimes suggest strange thoughts to the
wisest minds.

The well-timed hit on the lightning rod of
the not over-consistent George Forquer, in his
legislative canvass, recalls his clear and force-
ful side when his opponent assumed in public

the air of a superior and prodded young Lincoln on his coarse dress of homespun clothes,
with lack of experience and ability, and Lincoln in thoughtful manner replied and, review-
ing Forquer's follies and gullible nature as
the prey of seductive agents, said that while
he perhaps had many or most of the faults
ascribed to him, he was grateful that he " did
not have to erect a lightning rod over his home
to ward off the vengeance of an offended God "
as Forquer had.   As lightning rods were just
then introduced and under ban with the majority of the Illinois people Forquer was
silenced.

The Shields incident, when Lincoln was
forced as he thought to accept a challenge to
fight a duel, after writing the annonymous
letter as *a widow* from the "Lost Township,"
shows his final faith and reliance in sound every
day *man sense*.   James Shields was State Audi-
tor, and a rather excitable Irish gentleman from
Tyrone, Ireland, and took mortal offense at the
letters, as he imagined as a Democrat that they
reflected upon his personal honesty in office,
and no amount of persuasion by friends could

satisfy him of Lincoln's intended good nature, and so the challenge was forced upon Lincoln, and having choice of weapons, he, on the same principle which in later years actuated John F. Porter in Congress with Pryor, chose cavalry broadswords. The day came and the parties met—Shields, a little, large-headed and fiery man, and Lincoln of giant stature. At the final moment Shields gladly agreed to withdraw if his antagonist would assert that he only meant to make a political point as a Whig against a Democrat. Lincoln sensibly agreed. Asked later what he intended to do. had they fought, he said, "I should have used the advantage of my arms and legs and simply split him from head to heel."

It was nothing less than unique that upon his election to the Presidency he should appoint as his Cabinet and constant advisers the very men who were his opponents in the Republican National Convention for the nomination at Chicago in 1860, and yet by that act he had calmed and pacified all wounded aspirations, and though regarded as a dangerous move politically, it showed Lincoln's just and benevolent heart, his far-seeing judgment and his calm consciousness in his own ability to remain absolutely President and Commander-in-Chief of the Army and Navy of the United States.

The offense and as some felt, the ungrateful if not disloyal, conduct of his Secretary of the Treasury, Salmon P. Chase, in the treacherous storm and excitement of his second campaign in 1864, when Chase publicly became a candidate against his chief, again showed how truly great Lincoln was, and his words on this occasion and his subsequent act in appointing Secretary Chase, Chief Justice of the Supreme Court of the United States, proves him the towering political master and safe, unselfish patriot that he was.

The intense honesty shown in his settling accounts with the Government when postmaster at New Salem, when he months afterwards produced the exact amount to a dollar and a cent in the adjustment, and not only exact but the identical coins received by him in the office, all laid away sacredly awaiting the official accounting, although he had been sorely pressed in the meantime for money.

His stories have been retold, repeated and revamped until much falsehood has been mixed with original, all of which were pointed and practical and always prepared and thought out for purpose and to convince forcibly. A Lincoln story usually carries its own evidence of truth and originality. Sometimes they carried not only conviction but were calculated to cut or even humiliate if necessary. When his early antagonist at law, rather fresh and frothy, had talked at a rapid rate until he had tired court and jury, and for lack of facts sat down, to the relief of all, Lincoln in his thoughtful way said: "Your honor has observed the misfortune of the opposing counsel, as it is clear that he cannot work his mind and his voice at the same time, for the instant his tongue starts it goes so fast that the mind ceases to act. In fact he reminds me of the first steam vessel which appeared on the Sangamon river. It was noted for its efforts to navigate with ease, but it had a five-foot whistle and only a three-foot boiler, and every time they blew the whistle the boat had to stop still." This carries the true Lincoln brand.

The coarse jokes attributed to Lincoln never existed, and his intimates give testimony to that fact. In his associations with his Cabinet members he gave constant proof of his innate manliness, and nothing pleased him more in business meetings or official work than for all to call him Lincoln. He disliked to be called Mr. President or Your Excellency, but felt relief to be called Lincoln, and always spoke to his Ministers as Bates, Stanton, Chase and Seward, though he never missed seeing and appreciating the ludicrous and funny side to all things.

He was born a reasoner, and when a mere boy, after borrowing a copy of Weem's Life of Washington, and having left it in the log crevice in his Indiana home where it got soaked by a shower during the night, he agreed to work three days pulling corn for the close-fisted Crawford to settle the account; he first asked if the three days' work was to pay for the damage done the book or for the book

itself, and as Crawford thought the book of
no use, he said it would pay for the book,
and so Lincoln became owner of his first
actual book, and it proved a good bargain
too; and many a reader to-day would gladly
pay three hundred dollars for this same book
could they secure it for posterity.

His check for $5.00, made out while Presi-
dent, payable to "the one-legged colored man
or bearer," and which has been immortalized
by the Lincoln History Society of New York
City; his letter to the little boy who met him
on the street after he was nominated for President, spoke to him and shook hands with
him, and who was taunted by his playmates
in Springfield afterward for claiming Lincoln's acquaintance, until the great-hearted
man wrote in answer to the boy's childish
letter of appeal and stated over his signature
while President of the United States, that he
was glad to certify that he saw and remembered the boy and shook hands with him, and
thus the boy became a hero.

This same sincerity and frankness was ever
his strength and safety, and served as faith-

fully in the diplomacy of Nations and as easily and verily changed the fate of the American Continent, for while the trained and erudite Seward battled nervously with the ponderous and lugubrious ambiguities of Lord Palmerston, Lincoln had written a plain letter in plain and touching language to Queen Victoria direct, and appealed to her as a pure and noble woman to assure him in his trying ordeal against the sins of a century, that his efforts as a man threatened by rebellion yet seeking to maintain a friendly government in opposition to the spread of human slavery, should not be injured and weighted by England's enmity. On a bright Sunday morning he received her more than Queenly answer by mail, saying she realized the burdens and dangers to his government, and that slavery should not receive her aid or influence, and that the American government under his guidance would never need to fear from her people while she was acknowledged Queen of England. He had won by a man's sense what diplomacy never secured, and it was long afterward that Seward learned this great historic fact.

Lincoln's was the faith that never faltered, and was built on truth and sense.

Lincoln was pure in heart. He not only loved right, but he was grand enough to do right. He hated wrong and he did no wrong. He forgave to the last and loved forgiveness itself, and yet he needed little or none for himself. Hear his tender, fatherly voice as he whispers to little "Blossom" the pardon for her erring brother. See him as he dictates that immortal dispatch saving the tired soldier and sleeping sentinel, Scott, from an unmerited death. Think of his transcendent attitude in his position of almost unlimited power, as his acts of forgiveness fret and chafe the impatient generals who clamor for discipline at the expense of life, as he says: "*Gentlemen, I cannot take the lives of these boys who love their country but who have broken the rules of warfare in obedience to the demands of exhausted nature.*" His mantle has fallen upon no man. It is the heritage of America, the crown jewel of the world, and the hand of sacrilege alone shall ever touch it.

Let not the prude or the supercilious assume to blush at his humble, or even doubtful origin. Let them brush their dormant intelligence and remember who was William the Conqueror of England, and who was Charles Martel or "Charles the Hammer," who saved Christian civilization to Europe and who drove back the swelling tide of Moslemism in the decisive battle of Poitiers. Let them remember that *Abraham Lincoln was a man and as a man was the greatest compliment that has ever been given or paid to the human race*, and likewise that he was never the champion of the prude, the dude or the false; and aristocracy has no power to either harm or heighten his glory now, and neither prudes, puppets nor apologizers have any place in the following of his mighty train.

Lincoln could not sing a note, but music was to his soul a thing divine, and poetry and song may lay their garlands upon his tomb with perfect confidence for his character can absorb all their beauties and will glorify every author. His was the hand that wrote the request: "Please ask Philip Phillips to sing again to-night '*Your Mission*,' but do not say I said so."

Abraham Lincoln is the man who gave his first biographer a kindly, but knowing look when he found that he had stated that Lincoln had read Plutarch's Lives and had turned their sterling virtues to his own good account and character, who did not even correct the statement in the proof-sheet; but a week later when that same proof-sheet had been revised and was then ready for the printer, he, with equal kindness, and with a twinkling eye, informed his biographer, Mr. John Locke Scripps, that *in the meantime* he had read Plutarch from cover to cover and had not skipped even a single word, and that now the biography was correct and true and might be printed.

Here is a man who, while he may have said boyish things, and even followed the rougher customs of rollicking youth in the sturdy land of the pioneer, *yet in all the years of the prime of his manhood he was never known to say a foolish thing*. A man who constantly believed in himself and believed that he was being fitted for a great purpose and went on patiently, and not unconsciously, preparing to accept the highest post when the hour should strike. A man who was never surprised by the biggest events ; the patient, sad, and yet ever-rippling humorist who was great enough in the darkest hour to turn the serious incident into sunshine and laughter, thus giving to his nature that natural and joyous vent from the dangers of growing and crushing responsibility.

The man who never received or paid out an ill-earned or dishonest dollar in his whole life.

The man to whom criticism and discouragements served only as friction the better to propel the great engine of his mind as it tugged on the up-grade of events. The man who stood self-poised while he saw and realized that the die was being cast and saw the molten metal of his own wondrous history poured into the mould of immortality.

Surely Fate loved Lincoln, and in her longings she gave him the deathless kiss that he might never leave her.

While others quaked with fear at the gath-

ering storm he grasped the helm with giant
grip as the great Ship of State rode into the
roar and crash of the hurricane and held it
firm and safe until the lightnings had ceased
to play and until the vanishing clouds threw
their lessening shadows over her deck, and
until the big waves had done their worst and
until ripples only patted her storm-beaten
sides and the great white harbor was once
more in view with its sunshine and its peace.
Romance and miracle blend in the heavens
as the sun bursts upon the scene, for as the
last, long peal of thunder dies away in the
distance, and the Rainbow of Peace appears :
a sudden bolt from the clearing sky struck
him dumb and dead on the deck and *the Great
Loving Captain had gone to his reward in the
flower of his faith and in the full strength of
his giant manhood.*

It has been said that "God buries his workman but carries on his work," and this great
truth covers the life and martyrdom of Abraham Lincoln, the bravest, the most courageous,
the most useful, the kindest, the tenderest, *the
sweetest memory that has thus far appeared, in human form, within the Vestibule of Time.*

PART V.—ENLOE GENEALOGY.

Following we submit in the form of personal correspondence the result of the research of certain branches of the family. These letters were interchanged beginning in 1894, four years before the writer knew anything of this book, and ending with 1899 when the publication had quickened interest. They are printed verbatim from original manuscript forwarded us by the courtesy of Dr. I. N. Enloe, of Jefferson City, Mo., and to which we have alluded in our introduction. We invite the reader's careful study of our Enloe genesis throughout for in it history may have an honorable Scotch origin for Abraham Lincoln. In a future edition, more elaborate throughout, we purpose to include a full history of the Enloes. This edition with its predecessors are particularly meant hastily to recover and secure passing data upon the tradition :

JEFFERSON CITY, MO., June 23, 1899.
Dr. Thomas E. Enloe, Nashville, Tenn.:

DEAR SIR AND FRIEND :—In compliance

with your request and my promise made at
Nashville, August 29, 1898, while on my
way to Chickamauga—will now give you such
ready and accessible information as I possess
in regard to the Enloe family, by submitting
a copy (corrected and revised) of a letter written to Sam G. Enloe, of Mulberry Grove, Ill.,
bearing date of May 5, 1894, also his reply of
May 11, 1894, which read as follows:

JEFFERSON CITY, MO., May 5, 1894.
Sam G. Enloe, Mulberry Grove, Ill.:

DEAR SIR:—Your letter in regard to our
relationship, to hand and noted. Am satisfied we are of the same stock or family. Your
great-grandfather and my great-grandfather
were brothers, provided your father and B. A.
Enloe's father were cousins (that is first full
cousins), but am satisfied they must have been
second or third cousins.

Now, I will proceed to tell you my relationship to the 8th District Congressman of
Jackson, Tenn., and then you can figure out
our relationship. I am next to the youngest
son of Enoch Enloe, he the oldest son of

James Enloe, who was a full brother to Isaac
Enloe ; Isaac being the grandfather of Benj.
A. Enloe, the Congressman. Isaac and James
Enloe were both born in York county, South
Carolina, about 1791 and 1793 respectively.
They were reared by their half brother, Benjamin, the only brother they had, so far as I
know. So you can see from the above that I
and B. A. Enloe, of Jackson, Tenn., are great-
grand sons, he of Isaac and I of James Enloe.
They having a half brother by name of Ben,
and the three were the sons of Enoch Enloe.
My father was the youngest son of his father
by his last wife, an Irish woman by the name
of Jane McCord, whom he married long after
his first wife's death (whose maiden name I
never knew), and after his oldest son Ben,
had married and had quite a family.
Have often heard my grandfather, while
I was quite young, speak of his neph-
ews, some of whom were older than himself (sons of Ben), and with whom
he was raised. They were named Enoch,
Benjamin, Joel, Abraham, and others I do not
remember. His nephew Enoch, was older

than grandfather some few years, moved from Tennessee to Missouri a few years after grandfather did, which was in 1828, both settling in this, Cole county, near Russellville. Both lived to be eighty odd years old, and both raised large families. This nephew Enoch, I remember seeing the last years of his life, which was about 1874 (that being the year of his death). Grandfather, James Enloe, died in 1877. We always spoke of, and called this old nephew of grandfather's, Cousin Enoch, for he was my father's first half cousin.

Will now try to give the history beginning further back, and it's what I don't know about the Enloe family away back, that interests me most. From my oldest brother, James, who is about fifty-six years old, and who has heard grandfather speak of his ancestors during his life, I have information to this effect: It appears that the first of the Enloe stock or family, consisting of two brothers named Isaac and Enoch, both school teachers, settled in South Carolina, having previously taught school or lived for a short time in Maryland. This was some time near the middle of the eighteenth century. Both originally came from Scotland. My great-grandfather, Enoch, was one of these Enloe brothers. Both brothers, Isaac and Enoch, married in South Carolina and raised large families, Isaac's family became very wealthy and remained in that State. Enoch's family later on, say about 1808, moved to Tennessee. Am not able to go any farther back and am not positive that I am right about names, as it had always occurred to me that my great-grandfather's name was Isaac, until brother James, about two years ago, told me that his name was Enoch, and he ought to know, as he often talked to grandfather on the subject during his life-time.

In 1808 my grandfather moved with his half brother's family from South Carolina to Tennessee—to what part I don't know—both he and his brother Isaac, making Benjamin's home their home, until they were grown up, or nearly so.

My grandfather married Nancy Simpson, a sister of his brother Isaac's wife. Isaac and wife both died, leaving three sons, all or-

phans, named Benjamin, James and Joel.
Ben was raised by George Leslie, who was
his uncle by virtue of Leslie having married
a Simpson. Benjamin still lives in Tennessee and is the father of Benjamin A., the Congressman, Dr. Thomas and Dr. James, both
of Nashville, Tenn. James and Joel were
brought to Missouri by my grandfather,
who went back to Tennessee after them, after
the death of their father, and some years
after he had located in Missouri, and he raised
Joel, and Wm. Leslie raised James, who was
also an uncle by virtue of having married a
Simpson. James married his cousin, Polly
Enloe, who was a daughter of grandfather
(regardless of his, grandfather's protest),
and moved to Texas, raised, or partly raised,
a family, all of whom are now dead, including himself and wife. Joel married a Miss
Amos near Russellville, Mo., and died a few
years later, leaving one son and two daughters, all of whom are still living. His son is
named Isaac, and lives near Russellville, Mo.
Now, as to grandfather's family, I give
it last, as he was the youngest of the two

brothers. James Enloe was born in York County, South Carolina, February 19, 1793; moved with his brother Ben to Tennessee in 1808, was married about 1813 to Miss Nancy Simpson, and in 1830–31 moved to the State of Missouri, settling near Russellville in Cole County, where he entered land and farmed, devoting most of his attention to horses and politics, representing Cole County in the State Legislature once, and Moniteau, after it was cut off from Cole County, twice; raised a family of nine children, and died in 1877 at his youngest son Abraham's home in Moniteau County, where he was making his home. His children were named as follows: Enoch, John S., Hugh, Isaac, Jennie, Polly, Benjamin, William and Abraham.

My father Enoch was born in Barren County, Kentucky, where his father had moved temporarily May 19, 1814, he moved with his father to Missouri in 1830–31; married Miss Jane Murray in 1837, by which union fifteen children were born, named as follows: James, the oldest, now about 56 years old; Polly, Pollyann, and Nancy,

Thomas, Hugh, Maggie, Jennie, Barbara,. Henry, Enoch, Emma, John S., Isaac N.,. Sarah and Abraham. Polly, Pollyann, Nancy and Abraham died young.

My father died in 1873, mother in 1887. Brother James lives at Versailles, Morgan County, Mo., where his two oldest sons, H. King and Lone, are in the dry goods business. Brother Thomas lives near Russellville in Cole County, and is farming and owns the farm so long the home of his grandfather. Hugh L. Enloe lives in Russellville,. and is a dry goods merchant. Sister Maggie is the wife of A. J. Thompson, and they live in California, Mo. Sister Jennie on my father's old farm in Moniteau County, eight miles southeast of California, Mo., and is the wife of W. M. Gregory. Barbara lives near California and is the wife of W. H. Allen.. Henry Enoch Enloe lives in Fresno, Cal. Emma lives at Eugene, Oregon, and is the wife of George Cornell. Dr. John S. Enloe, has been practicing medicine at St. Thomas, Mo., twenty miles south of here, but has sold out. His wife and three children are with her mother, and he is now in New York City, attending a post-graduate course of lectures at the Polyclinic Hospital School of Medicine. He will likely locate in the State again upon his return. I come next in order. I was born in 1860 in Moniteau County, on the farm where nearly all the children were raised, located eight miles southeast of California. Graduated from the Missouri Medical College, St. Louis, class of 1883, located at St. Thomas, Mo., where I practiced till October, 1889, when I sold out to my brother John, went to New York, spending part of the winter there, attending a post-graduate course, after which I located in Jefferson City, where I have practiced ever since, married Miss Rebecca J. Short, October 12, 1886. Our family consists of two girls and two boys. The oldest six years old and the youngest ten months, name Loyce, Ada, David and Justin. I was elected Coroner of this county on the Republican ticket in 1884, and defeated for Representative of this county in 1888.

Old cousin Enoch Enloe's family are, as a rule, Democrats, while the descendants of grandfather, with the exception of John S., his second son, are all strong in the Republican·faith.

Will state that I was both pleased and surprised to receive a letter from you, not knowing that such a man was in existence; also glad to note, judging from indications, that you are prospering and right in politics. Would be pleased to have you visit me, and there are other Enloes in Missouri who would make you feel at home among them, should you ever see fit to pay this section of the country a visit. Now, take your time and give me all the information you have in regard to your family, and the same will be appreciated by me.   Very respectfully yours,

                                    I. N. ENLOE.

MULBERRY GROVE, ILL., May, 1893.

Dr. I. N. Enloe:

DEAR SIR :—Yours of the 5th to hand and in reply will say that I am not well posted on the genealogy of the Enloe family, but I know from the names that you give me, that you are of the same stock and started from the same section of the country, York county, South Carolina. You say that you don't think that my father could have been a full cousin to the father of B. A. Enloe, the Tennessee congressman. I will give the genealogy as given by my father in the history of Bond county, Ill. He says that his father was the son of Isaac Enloe, a Scotsman who came to this country from Scotland near the middle of, or about the year 1750. There were two brothers, as you say, Isaac and Enoch. My father's name was James. He was born in 1803 in York county, South Carolina. His father's name was Isaac and he was the son of one of the original Scotch brothers that came to this country from Scotland about 1750, and served in the Revolutionary war. My grandfather had a brother named Gilbert that never left South Carolina, so far as I know. He was there and still living in 1868. My grandfather left South Carolina in about 1768 and came to Davidson county, Tenn., where he taught school for some time, and you will find that he is given quite a prominent place in the history of that county, as an educator.

He left Tennessee with his family and arrived in Madison county, Ill., in 1816. Moved to Bond county, Ill., in the year 1818. My grandfather was a surveyor and teacher in this county from 1820 until he became too old to follow these vocations further. He died in this county as near as I can remember about 1852. He was a Presbyterian in religious belief as most of the Enloes are, I believe. If my grandfather ever had any brothers except Gilbert, I never heard my father say anything about them, and don't think that there were any sisters of grandfather and Gilbert; never heard of any. The names of my father's brothers were Ezekiel, James, Enoch, Nathaniel and Isaac. Isaac died in this county only a few years ago near 75 years old. Enoch lived and died in Wisconsin. There are none of Asahel Enloe's sons or daughters now living. I have two brothers living here, I. N. and E. L. Enloe. I. N. is older than myself and was also in the army during the war, as also was my youngest brother, E. L., and myself. Both rose to the command of our companies. I went through

without being wounded, but I. N. was shot
through the leg, in front of Atlanta. All
the Enloes here are Republicans of the
strictest sect, except E. L. He is a Democrat. During the war we captured an Enloe
near Holly Springs, Miss., and I had never
heard of him before, but I knew him as soon
as I saw him. He was named Nathaniel
Enloe, and was a cousin of James Enloe, the
Presbyterian preacher that lived at Holly
Spring during the war. I have also heard
my father and uncles speak about Ben and
Joel Enloe, who lived in the southern part of
the State. Ben used to represent his county
in the Illinois Legislature when the capital of
our State was at Vandalia, in Fayette county,
only ten miles from my place. If I mistake
not they lived in White county, and were both
very large men and both used to be at Vandalia during the sessions of the legislature.
Ben would raise a row in the legislature or on
the streets, and Joel would do his fighting.
As Joel was a man that weighed about 250
pounds, and was stout, he nearly always came
out all right. I have heard my father tell

about Ben having his fun with our representative, Col. Bentley of Greenville; also with
Col. McGlouthlin, of Vandalia. I think that
Ben was there before the time of Lincoln and
Douglas, but these times are now passed. I
saw by the papers during the war that there
was an Enloe that was a member of the legislature of your State, called to his door and
shot by a band of bushwhackers, as his wife
stood by his side. I don't remember what
county he represented, but think it was St.
Genevieve county. So it appears that at least
most of the Enloes in the North were loyal
and true. Every Enloe of the name here
that could go was in the service. I have been
since the war, county commissioner, police
judge of this city, mayor four times, have been
State delegate to the Republican conventions
before, and am a delegate this year also, and
I think beyond a doubt we will nominate a
ticket that will win this fall. I was also postmaster here for a term of four years.

Well, wishing you success in life, I will
close. Would be pleased to hear from you at
any time.   SAM G. ENLOE.

I herewith send you a copy of a letter re-cently received from J. E. Enloe, Whittier, N. C.

This branch of the family I had never been able to trace beyond Gilbert, who was a son of the original Enloes of 1750. This letter tells the story, and gives a pointer that will enable you to become reconciled, as to the meager reports, you have no doubt often heard, that Lincoln was the son of one Abraham Enloe.

This tradition is backed with such strong circumstantial evidence that it convicts.

The tradition came to Missouri from Kentucky in 1828, and 1835, in an intensely sub-dued form, but was discussed in such a way during the war that the younger generation obtained an inkling of it.

The Enloes, Leslies, Simpsons, Shorts, Van Pools are the people I have reference to. They lived at that time in Kentucky, about twenty miles from where Columbus is now located. They were neighbors also in Missouri and but few of the old ones are now living. The J. F. E. letter reads as follows:

WHITTIER, N. C., June 3, 1899.

Dr. I. N. Enloe, Jefferson City, Mo. :

DEAR SIR :—Your letter was forwarded to me from Cherokee where I once lived. In reply to your letter I will say that I am sure that we are the same stock. From the best information I have, there were three brothers of the original Enloes who came from the Old Country. They made their first stop in Maryland, where one of them stayed and raised a family. One of them emigrated to York District, South Carolina; this was my great-grandfather; I think his name was Gilbert. My grandfather, Abraham Enloe, came over to Rutherford county, North Carolina, and married a Miss Egerton. He afterwards moved, first above the Indian Mission in Bucombe county, then to Ocona Lufta River, where he resided till his death. He raised nine sons and seven daughters. The other brother of my great-grandfather and one of the original three went to middle Tennessee and settled. One of his descendants, B. A. Enloe, represented the Eighth Tennessee District, as you state in your letter. Some of the Yorkville branch of the family moved to Georgia, and elsewhere. In Georgia they spell their name Inlow. My father is the only one living out of sixteen. He is in his 89th year.

I have always heard that Abe Lincoln was a son of my grandfather, Abraham Enloe.

There is a book now written that gives a good history of the Enloe and Lincoln tradition. It is by Jas. H. Cathey, of Sylva, N. C.

Yours very truly,

J. F. ENLOE.

[J. F. Enloe is undoubtedly mistaken about a brother of his great-grandfather, and one of the original three, moving to Tennessee. This Tennessee immigrant was either a brother or cousin of his grandfather—Abraham Enloe. He is also mistaken about Gilbert Enloe being his great-grandfather. Gilbert Enloe was the son of Isaac Enloe and belonged to the same generation as J. F. Enloe's grandfather and was the cousin of his grandfather and, doubtless, the son of Enoch Enloe, the other of the original Scotch brothers.—THE AUTHOR.]

I have never had the pleasure of meeting Sam G. Enloe, yet I am satisfied he is an Enloe of the old type. In a letter dated May 28, 1899, he states in substance, that he is fifty-nine years of age, six feet and one-half inches, weight one hundred and eighty. I herewith (without his permission, but knowing it will not offend him) submit to you another letter recently received from him :

MULBERRY GROVE, ILL., June 6, 1899.

Dr. I. N. Enloe:

DEAR SIR :—Yours of the 5th received. At first I will give you the names and ages of my sisters and brothers : first, Nancy A. Enloe, born 1830—69 years old ; Mary E. Enloe, born 1832—67 years old ; William B. Enloe, born 1834—65 years old; Isaac N. Enloe, born 1836—63 years old ; Violet R. Enloe, born 1838—61 years old; Samuel G. Enloe, born 1840—59 years old; Emery L. Enloe, born 1842—57 years old ; Harriette N. Enloe, born 1845—54 years old; Louisa I. Enloe, born 1847—52 years old ; James S. Enloe, born 1849—50 years old ; Cynthy E. Enloe, born

1851—48 years old; Emily Zantavia Enloe, born 1856—43 years old. Of these Nancy A., William B., Violet R., Harriet N., James S., and Emily Z., are dead, six dead and six living. Father and mother both dead; mother died in 1871 and father in 1884. Father had five sisters and brothers, and what I can learn of the stock all over the country, they always have been and still are, very prolific. I have but one child, Ernest R. Enloe, born 1872, and now in his twenty-seventh year, he is married and has two children, Loucile E. Enloe, and Rachel Enloe, both girls, one four years old and the other two years old. This is correct so far as my father's and my own families are concerned.

SAM G. ENLOE.

I think beyond a doubt that J. F. Enloe is mistaken as to Gilbert Enloe being one of the old ones that came from Scotland with Enoch and Isaac, but Gilbert was the son of Isaac and was a brother of my grandfather Asahel, and uncle of my father. I have heard my father tell of old Uncle Gilbert many a time, and I have talked with a man since the war who came from there since the war, and he told me that he was well acquainted with old Uncle Gilbert. I don't think that Gilbert was as old as my grandfather, but still he was old enough to be the father of J. F.'s grandfather. So I think J. F. and I are of the same brand of the family. I guess that B. A. Enloe, of Tennessee, is of the Enoch brand. There was during the war a James Enloe near Holly Springs, Miss. He was a Presbyterian minister, and there were other Enloes lived there. We captured one named Nathaniel Enloe, and I knew that he was an Enloe as soon as I saw him, and he knew me although we had never seen or heard of each other before. We shook hands whilst both Fed. and Confed. looked on, but all noted the resemblance. He claimed he and Jim both to be cousins of my father. There are also two doctors I think living in Nashville, Tenn., and there used to be a Presbyterian preacher who lived in Murfreesboro, Tenn. Our folks of the old stock were all Presbyterians. The Abraham spoken of, I think ·by J. F., was the father of Wesley, a grandfather of J. F., that would make Gilbert J. F.'s great-grandfather, provided Abraham was Gilbert's son, which I think he was. I have written to South Carolina and North Carolina both for information, and when I get it I will let you know, but I guess that you have no doubt noticed the marked personal resemblance of Abraham Lincoln and the Enloes. Most of the Enloes are tall, raw-boned, high cheeks and immense ears, all but me, and I got mine froze off during the war. We are all of Southern origin, I on both sides; my father having been born in South Carolina and my mother, who was a Bradford, a sister of Judge James Bradford, was born in Kentucky. She was a cousin of the Mayor Bradford that was slain after capture of the Rebs at Fort Dillon in 1863. If, at sometime when you are making a business trip to St. Louis, you will let me know, I will meet you there if I can and get better acquainted with you. I think that I have given you the facts as I understood them, so I will close. Hoping to hear from you often, I remain as ever,

SAM G. ENLOE.

It appears that the two original brothers were pioneers of South Carolina about the year 1750 where they both died. Their descendants being among the earlier settlers of North Carolina, Tennessee, Kentucky, Illinois, Missouri, Texas, and California, some drifting to Georgia and Wisconsin.

They were possessed of more than ordinary physical ability, honesty, determination and endurance. Physical ability, determination and endurance are attested by the prompt manner in which they pushed forward into new country, facing strange and partially civilized people, and poverty. As to honesty, the assertion goes with my convictions.

Joel and Benjamin Enloe, spoken of by Sam G., in his letter as being at the Legislature of Illinois prior to 1860, were the sons of Benjamin.

Benjamin was the old half brother of Isaac and James, our grandfathers. Isaac and James grew up wilh Joel and Ben and their brothers.

I have often heard my grandfather talk about Joel's fights in Kentucky and Tennessee. We knew that Ben had located in Illinois but

did not know what had become of Joel until
Sam G. related the characteristics of Joel and
Ben of Illinois. Hence, I take it, they are
the same people.

These letters cover the ground in a way, and
I trust they will be of interest to you. Changes
are always occurring as time rolls on. But
so slight in this case with our family that the
mention of the same would be of little interest, to you.

My family now consist of Loyce, age 11,
Ada 9, David 7, Justin 5, Robert and Roscoe
(twins), age 3 years. Brother John is now
located in Southeast Missouri, at Greenville,
Wayne county.

Have been feeling duty bound to write you
on this subject for quite a while, but busy pro-
fessionally, and dreading the task, anyway, I
have deferred it from time to time.

This leaves all well. With kindest regards
I remain, yours truly,

I. N. ENLOE.

THE END.

CPSIA information can be obtained
at www.ICGtesting.com
Printed in the USA
BVHW041600060620
581010BV00007BA/47